THE
SHIFTING FRONTIERS
OF ACADEMIC
DECISION MAKING

THE
SHIFTING FRONTIERS
OF ACADEMIC
DECISION MAKING

Responding to New Priorities,
Following New Pathways

Edited by
Peter D. Eckel

AMERICAN COUNCIL ON EDUCATION
PRAEGER
Series on Higher Education

Library of Congress Cataloging-in-Publication Data

The shifting frontiers of academic decision making : responding to new priorities, following new pathways / edited by Peter D. Eckel.
     p. cm.—(ACE/Praeger series on higher education)
  Includes index.
  ISBN 0–275–98792–2
  1. Universities and colleges—Administration. 2. Educational leadership. 3. Decision making. I. Eckel, Peter D. II. Series: American Council on Education/Praeger series on higher education.
LB2341.S465   2006
378.1'01—dc22   2006015705

British Library Cataloguing in Publication Data is available.

Library of Congress Catalog Card Number: 2006015705
ISBN: 0–275–98792–2

First published in 2006

Praeger Publishers, 88 Post Road West, Westport, CT 06881
An imprint of Greenwood Publishing Group, Inc.
www.praeger.com

Printed in the United States of America

The paper used in this book complies with the Permanent Paper Standard issued by the National Information Standards Organization (Z39.48–1984).

10 9 8 7 6 5 4 3 2 1

CONTENTS

PREFACE

The test of a first-rate intelligence is the ability to hold two opposed
ideas in mind at the same time and still retain the ability to
function.

—F. Scott Fitzgerald

The challenges facing colleges and universities today push campus leaders
to simultaneously hold two competing conceptions of academic decision
making. On the one hand, academic decision making invokes higher education's history and traditions of shared governance, collegiality, and a community of
scholars. The image is one of academic peers coming together to address perennial
questions such as what should be taught, what priorities should the institution
pursue, and what policies and structures will allow the institution to fulfill its mission. However, on the other hand, the changing environment in which higher
education finds itself—with increased competition, fiscal constraints, privatization, new conceptions of accountability, and the changing relationships between
government (both state and federal) institutions, among other challenges—suggests that academic decision making is the dynamic set of processes institutions
use to address such challenges. Academic decision making may be the domain of
traditional faculty senates, but it also involves ad hoc processes and nontraditional
players. It is about deliberation, examination, and debate, but it is also about
responsiveness, opportunity, and agility. It is about tradition, academic values,
and scholarly community, and it is about new ways of doing business, leveraging
institutional resources, and capitalizing on institutional strengths. Academic decision making is all of these things at the same time.

This book explores these opposing ideas about academic decision making. It is about the decision-making traditions that have long made American higher education strong. But it is also a book about the new challenges and how institutions are responding. It looks at decision-making issues such as the continuing expansion of new decision makers into campuses processes and the opportunities and difficulties of developing and using new and familiar decision-making structures. It investigates the new challenges institutions are facing and how colleges and universities are invoking familiar as well as new but accepted processes to address them. Thus, this work explores elements found along the frontiers of academic decision making.

The idea for this book surfaced at a meeting of higher education scholars. Independently, individuals were thinking about aspects of contemporary campus governance—activist boards, commercial activities, ad hoc decision-making bodies, joint academic programs, tensions between research centers and institutes, and traditional academic departments—that, when viewed together, suggested that the interesting questions regarding academic decision making were no longer about faculty-administrator tensions, the role of unions and senates, or how to make campus decisions faster and better. Each person was identifying various elements that make up the new frontiers of academic decision making. This book, by pulling those disparate topics together, illuminates a changing world for institutional decision makers.

The book contains eight chapters. The first chapter, by Peter Eckel and Adrianna Kezar, frames the book by providing a conceptual understanding of academic decision making. It explores the challenges to academic decision making created by an institution's steadfast organizational structures—such as faculty and administrator competing sources of authority, its loosely coupled nature, and its latent functions of decision-making processes—and the changing environment. It is the intersection of these two phenomena that shape (and frustrate) decision making on campus.

The second chapter, by Bill Mallon, explores the continuing rise of research institutes and centers and what they mean for academic decision making. In an era of "big" biomedical science, the higher education community increasingly views scientific research and the intellectual property it generates as keys to university prosperity and prestige. These interdisciplinary research centers and institutes continue to become a favored mechanism for the advancement of these goals. Center directors often are big-name scholars who control significant sums of funding, faculty lines, and formal and informal lines of authority. Based on survey and case study research, this chapter explores the tensions created and resolved between those "suburbs" of the university—the research institutes and centers—and the university's academic "city-center," the traditional department.

The third chapter, by Jared Bleak, further explores the challenges to academic decision making that the pursuit of revenue creates. Rather than research institutes, he focuses on commercial academic activities, particularly for-profit subsidiaries created to market and deliver distance education. To many faculty, these companies are the embodiment of destructive trends at work. In addition to attempting to leverage the curriculum for explicit monetary gain, they can be perceived to challenge faculty prerogative over curricular decisions and change the ground rules by which such decisions are made. This chapter draws upon several case studies of both successful and failed efforts of academic commercialization to illustrate the challenges of decision making according to the market. The chapter pursues the important and timely question of whether it is possible for higher education to do business like a business—a trend afoot in the academy for good or bad—and still retain core academic values and cultures.

Peter Eckel contributes the fourth chapter that explores the challenges that joint academic programs create for academic governance. As institutions seek ways to minimize academic and instructional expenditures, they may consider developing and delivering new degree programs through a variety of partnerships and alliances. Such shared approaches allow partners to share costs, build upon strengths, and distribute risks. However, as everyone knows, curricular decisions can be complex and contentious on any campus, particularly during times of fiscal constraint. Joint programs add an additional layer of complexity by involving faculty and administrators from multiple institutions and complicating the delivery decisions faced by any one program.

Matt Hartley and Simi R. Wilhelm Shah suggest that the senate and standing campus committees are not the only groups responsible for making academic decisions. They focus on ad hoc campus-wide task forces. Unencumbered by day-to-day decision-making responsibilities and free of institutional histories, task forces may increasingly be important means to render academic decisions. This chapter examines whether such arrangements are a legitimate means of producing faster decision making, or whether they constitute an "end run" around traditional forms of governance and how institutions can effectively create and use such approaches.

Adrianna Kezar, in the sixth chapter, looks at the changing role of students in academic decision making. For the most part, the ways in which students actually participate in campus-level decision making are undocumented systemically. Kezar draws upon a variety of case studies to present various approaches that are appearing. She argues that higher education may be entering a new period—following in loco parentis and student activism—in how it involves students in institutional decisions. As more and more campuses include students on institutional decision-making bodies, from search committees to presidential advisory boards, they are melding important philosophies about the role of students on campus and the educational opportunities institutions should be providing for their students.

The seventh chapter, by Dennis Gayle, shifts the focus from the roles that individuals play, or the types of activities on that frontier, to the pervasive ways in which technology is shaping decision making. He argues that educational and communication technologies (ECTs) are increasingly affecting academic decision making as they alter aspects of campus administration, research, teaching, and learning. Technology puts new issues on institutional agendas, such as those regarding intellectual property, privacy, and security, but it also shapes how decisions occur. As Gayle argues, technology both drives and mediates decision making on campus.

The final chapter further expands the focus of academic decision making to include trustees. Michael Bastedo's chapter addresses the increasing phenomenon of activist trustees and explores their impact on academic decision making. The chapter provides perspectives from both trustees and public college leaders and offers suggestions for improving the vital relationship between trustees and campus leaders. He further argues that what is really at stake, beyond the political agendas involved, is that such behavior has the potential to significantly change the power dynamic between key institutional decision makers. It is not the content of their message, but how their actions create a different set of ground rules for faculty and administrators.

Bringing these chapters together in a single place amplifies the changes occurring in higher education. It calls attention to the ways in which academic decision making is evolving in light of a dynamic environment. The individual chapters are strong, and each advances our understanding and poses questions for campus decision makers of all types to consider.

I thank the contributors for their good work. They wrote careful arguments, were diligent about deadlines, and were open to comments and feedback (some even were appreciative). They made my job as editor much easier and highly enjoyable. As editor, I thank Susan Slesinger of Greenwood Publishing for her assistance with this effort, as well as Wendy Bresler, Madeleine Green, and Mike Baer at the American Council on Education for their encouragement and support in bringing this book to light. As an author, I want to thank Adrianna Kezar and Bill Mallon for their helpful comments and encouragements, as well as Britney Affolter-Caine for her initial efforts on curricular joint ventures. Finally, thank you to Erin Rooney-Eckel for her patience as I obsessed about this book, my chapters, and its deadlines.

CHAPTER 1

The Challenges Facing Academic Decision Making: Contemporary Issues and Steadfast Structures

Peter D. Eckel
American Council on Education

Adrianna Kezar
University of Southern California

Many leaders of colleges and universities find themselves wading carefully through a swamp of new decision-making challenges, and they often find themselves slipping. They may know how to address historic questions such as which students to admit, what programs to offer, who shall teach, what research should be pursued, and where to invest scare resources. However, new issues have worked themselves onto institutional agendas that reflect changing times, such as concerns over ownership of intellectual property, the privatization of public institutions, the appropriateness of entrepreneurial activities, internationalization, technology, activist boards, revenue-driven athletics programs, merit-based aid recruitment strategies, competition and reputation rankings, and public accountability, to name a few. These contemporary issues call for new and unfamiliar decisions, add complexities into the decision-making processes, expand the locations throughout campus where key institutional decisions are made, and bring new players with strengthened influence into the mix. Perennial questions associated with shared governance, such as who has the expertise, authority, or responsibility to make a particular decision, what processes should be used for which decisions, what should be the amount of involvement (or review or approval), and how long decisions should take, haunt both the long-standing and new decision-making challenges. For many institutions, the stakes are high as institutions find themselves in increasingly competitive environments with little room for trial and error and even less room for mistakes or indecision.

As academic decision making becomes more complex, the questions are: How are institutions keeping pace, and how do they make good decisions? Institutions may develop new decision-making strategies that are tightly linked to traditional governance processes. However, at other times, the decisions may require very different processes that may compete with or contradict well-established ways of making academic decisions. The lack of information, the ambiguity of the pressing situations, the speed at which decisions are required, and the sheer number of decisions may lead some decision makers to rush down unfamiliar pathways without laying the proper groundwork or to create processes that are so far afield from the expected ways of making decisions that they alienate important campus stakeholders. The result could put the institution into gridlock or undermine the decision makers' own leadership credibility.

The academy, for the most part, is highly participative and grounded in a history of collegiality, shared governance, and professional prerogative. It is through campus governance structures that faculty, administrators, and trustees (and sometimes students and others) interact to make academic decisions. Much of the current assumptions about academic decision making are shaped by the 1966 *Statement on Government of Colleges and Universities* (American Association of University Professors [AAUP], 1995), jointly formulated by the AAUP, the American Council on Education (ACE), and the Association of Governing Boards of Universities and Colleges (AGB). The *Statement*, although not intended to serve as a blueprint for institutional decision making, outlines roles for faculty, administrators, and trustees in governance decisions. For example, it suggests that issues such as managing the endowment fall to the trustees, maintaining and creating new resources to the president, and developing the curriculum to the faculty. Not all decisions neatly fall into the domain of one of the three groups. It notes that much of institutional governance is (or should be) conducted jointly. Questions over general education policy, the framing and execution of long-range plans, budgeting, and presidential selection should be decided jointly.

The *Statement* in practice does not work so smoothly. Different groups can too easily make the case that a specific decision is its domain. For example, how can an institution determine if offering a highly marketable joint master's degree program with a foreign university is the responsibility of the president, who, according to the *Statement*, is responsible for maintaining and creating new resources; the faculty, who are responsible for the curriculum; or the trustees, who oversee the institution's strategy and long-range objectives? Or is this new initiative a joint effort? And, if so, is participation among the groups equal? The answers often depend on where one's perspective sits. When high stakes are involved or the decisions are unfamiliar, the probability of conflict over who decides tends to rise.

Any experienced campus leader knows there is no shorter path to institutional paralysis than to tap the wrong decision processes, overlook important options, not involve the right people, or follow procedures perceived to be illegitimate for their purpose. However, with the proper attention, institutional leaders can develop responsive academic decision-making processes, ones that accommodate the changing environment and meet contemporary organizational needs.

This opening chapter sets the stage for the chapters that follow, which explore the changing higher education environment and how institutional decision-making efforts are responding. It outlines key environmental changes that affect academic decision making, describes structural elements that influence how decisions are made, and offers suggestions for campus decision makers. Finally, it concludes with a discussion of effectiveness. These elements serve as a foundation for the remaining chapters.

THE CHANGING CONTEXT FOR ACADEMIC DECISION MAKING

In the early 1980s, shared governance was described tongue-in-cheek, in a fable by Baldridge (1982), as the lost "Magic Kingdom" facing an onslaught of challenges, such as the reduced role and scope of the academic department, the rise of a professionalized university administration, tensions between senates and faculty unions, and the centralization of decision making, which work against collegial academic decision making. Many issues that Baldridge described as affecting shared governance 25 years ago are still very much present; however, the past quarter century has seen additionally significant challenges, and new ones are poised on the horizon as well. Brief overviews follow of four changes that have the potential to reshape academic decision making.

The Changing Relationship between States and Their Institutions

For most institutions, the long-established relationships between state governments and their public colleges and universities are being revisited, with repercussions for decision making in both public and independent institutions. The old relationship, where state governments served as the primary source of financial support and played an important hand in setting university policy, is at a minimum being rethought, and, in extreme cases, some say abandoned altogether (Newman, Couturier, & Scurry, 2004; Yudof, 2002). As the relationships are recast, new notions of autonomy and accountability are appearing, typically accompanied with significant downward changes in public dollars (Kane & Osgood, 2003), which leave institutions needing to raise additional resources elsewhere through a range of traditional and novel strategies. The result is that public colleges and universities find themselves in a highly market-driven environment that puts new, additional pressures on academic decision makers.

A key element of this changing relationship is the increased focus by policy makers and the public on accountability and governance transparency. Institutions are no longer simply trusted to deliver their missions. Instead they must demonstrate value for public investment. Calls for accountability ring from statehouses across the nation. A recent national commission composed of higher education, business, and political leaders called for "a better system of accountability that will put more emphasis on successful student learning and high quality research ... and provide parents, students, concerned citizens and policymakers with the answers to reasonable questions regarding costs, ... availability of required courses, what students are learning, and graduation rates" (State Higher Education Executive Officers, 2005, pp. 6–7). Furthermore, corporate scandals, such as those involving executives at Enron, Tyco, and Arthur Andersen, to name a few, have increased public skepticism about governance, and amplified calls to hold decision makers in all types of organizations, for-profit and nonprofit, more publicly accountable.

The Growing Presence and Strength of the Marketplace

The flipside of declining public support is a rise in market forces as institutions compete for new resources. With declining proportions of state funds, institutions pursue strategies to make up for lost revenue. They pursue activities and strategies—both academic and auxiliary—they hope will generate a sizable return on investments (Bok, 2003; Hearn, 2003). They have exponentially increased their patents and licenses and developed new units and offices as well as research parks and partnerships devoted to technology transfer for economic gain, among other strategies. The result is a close relationship with a marketplace that favors and encourages (as well as rewards) activities and research in certain market-sensitive fields, such as engineering, applied natural science, and agricultural science over other programs such as humanities disciplines, as well as activities that result in more students (particularly those that can afford to pay the high tuition prices), new contracts and partnership agreements, and enhanced research programs (Slaughter & Leslie, 1997). Issues such as intellectual property, faculty work-for-hire, and the proprietariness of knowledge will require focused institutional attention. Some of these undertakings may have significant commercial value but may not directly advance institutional missions.

The rise of the market has the potential to change internal institutional dynamics. Colleges and universities may increasingly look to adapt practices and values from the for-profit sector that challenge long-held institutional relationships and expectations (Birnbaum, 2001). In some instances, departments, research centers, and other units able to generate revenue will set their own rules and demand greater autonomy because of their newfound economic clout. For example, Kirp (2003) describes the deal made by the Darden Graduate School of Business Administration with its parent institution, the University of Virginia. The business school determines its own fees and decides how many professors to hire and sets their salaries independent of the university pay structure. It has its own foundation and keeps 90 percent of the funds it raises. It even has its own Web site, symbolic of an autonomy that other academic units at the university do not have.

Given the current drive for resources, institutional decision makers will face two central and weighty questions: First, how do institutions seeking new sources of revenue balance the advancement of their social missions with the pursuit of additional resources that might distort the mission? And second, are market-orientated changes strengthening nonprofit colleges and universities and making them more effective in meeting society's needs, or are they weakening them, diverting their efforts, leading to counterproductive behavior? (Weisbrod, 1998).

The University as a Global Entity

Historically, colleges and universities have had an international component to their missions—offering courses on international issues, studying different nations and cultures, teaching languages, engaging in development work, educating foreign nationals and sending students abroad, and collaborating internationally on scholarship. However, globalization puts new issues on the table as it moves rapidly from a peripheral focus to a central one. An increased international presence means that more and more institutions are concerned not only with adding international components into their curricula and hiring and promotion practices, but with establishing a presence across borders as well. For example, they enter into partnerships with institutions abroad to facilitate student and faculty exchange, deliver joint programs with international partners, supplement their on-campus academic programs by adding international dimensions, and take their internationally market-focused programs to other nations, where they confront a different group of competitors.

Global trends and issues put new topics on institutional agendas as campus leaders consider strategies thought far-fetched a few years ago, such as opening international branch campuses, requiring all undergraduate students to study abroad, or complying with international trade agreements that cover education as a marketable service. They expand their staffs with another set of key managerial professionals who have international (and international business) experience, involving them in key strategic decisions. Partnerships with foreign providers further create avenues for faculty and staff from other institutions to participate in academic programmatic decisions.

The Changing Academic Workforce

Finally, important internal changes are occurring that will affect academic decision making. None is more powerful to academic decision making than the changing nature of the academic workforce. Academic employment trends have changed significantly in the last 30 years. The proportion of full-time faculty continues to decrease dramatically at research, liberal arts, and comprehensive institutions, and community colleges have long drawn heavily upon a contingent faculty workforce. In the 1970s, tenure track faculty numbered almost 80 percent of the faculty on these campuses and by recent count are less than 50 percent (Anderson, 2002; Kezar, 2001). Between 1981 and 1999, the number of part-time faculty grew by 79 percent (Anderson, 2002). Based upon 1998 data, part-time faculty made up the majority of new hires made within the past five years, and in community colleges, 80 percent of new hires were part-timers (Anderson, 2002).

Additionally, the nature of faculty work continues to change, making the service required for effective governance an increasingly low priority. Research on the professoriate continually demonstrates that faculty spend the great majority of their time engaged in scholarship and many believe this to be their most important task (Fairweather, 1996). Related to trends in privatization, another trend is for faculty to be increasingly rewarded for entrepreneurialship, adding additional dimensions to their scholarship and grant writing. Finally, additional public pressure to focus on teaching and student learning outcomes means that campus service is pushed even further down the priority list. The result is that the tradition of shared governance may be threatened if faculty members do not have the time and inclination to participate in governance of emerging institutional operations and directions.

THE ORGANIZATIONAL REALITIES OF ACADEMIC DECISION MAKING

To craft academic decision-making processes and structures that address today's challenges, campus leaders might find themselves wanting to alter current structures or develop new ones. However, by tinkering with the wrong elements or with the right elements but in the wrong ways, leaders can easily develop processes that on the surface may seem like plausible solutions, but in the end actually impede the institution's ability to make good decisions. The result can be short-term inconveniences. Or, on the other hand, their actions may result in long-term harm that lasting institutional memories may make difficult to correct. Although institutions are unique in many ways, most (nonprofit) public and independent institutions share some similar organizational characteristics that shape academic decision making.

The organizational characteristics particular to colleges and universities can help explain a number of institutional behaviors. For instance, conflicts between faculty and administrators can seemingly come from nowhere. What should be simple frequently (and unexplainably) becomes compounded by the current preferences, pet ideas, and personal agendas of those involved, and made into a highly complex undertaking. At the same time, what should be complex ends up being simple because no one decided to pay attention to the particular issue. People see decisions as opportunities to participate in the life of the campus, as a retreat from boredom, or as ways to establish (or advance) their status, among other things. Even then, decisions that seem to have limited focus can affect the institution beyond the outcomes they render. The following sections further describe some of these organizational phenomena common to colleges and universities that influence academic decision making.

Dual Sources of Authority

Colleges and universities comprise two competing sources of authority—bureaucratic (or administrative) and professional—that frequently come into conflict around academic decisions (Birnbaum, 1988). Unlike other organizations in which those at the top of the hierarchy make key decisions, in colleges and universities, these responsibilities are shared (or divided depending upon one's perspective) mostly between faculty and administrators, each acting on their own source of organizational authority. The administrator's bureaucratic authority stems from the organization's hierarchy and structure and from the legal rights of administrators to set direction, control and monitor budgets, develop institution strategy, hire and terminate employees, develop and implement policies, and assess progress toward objectives and priorities. This source of influence is important for organizations to run effectively. At the same time, the faculty has its own source of authority, which is derived from their specialized training and professional expertise essential to their fundamental role in delivering core organizational functions (Mintzberg, 1993). Not just anyone can teach about high-particle physics or about eighteenth-century Japanese printmaking, or conduct advanced chemical engineering research.

Professional and bureaucratic authority come into contact and conflict in campus decision making, with each side asserting its rights to decide a particular issue. Often the result is that no clear decision is rendered and much attention is given to deciding who should be deciding. As Henry Rosovsky, former dean of Harvard College, says, "governance concerns power: who is in charge; who makes decisions; who has a voice, and how loud that voice is" (1990, p. 261). Much time and energy in campus decision making is spent negotiating among the various sources of organizational authority and not always on resolving the issues at hand. Regardless of how much effort goes into defining appropriate roles for various parties, the ambiguities of institutional life mean that negotiations will inevitably occur.

Loosely Coupled Units

Colleges and universities are organized in ways in which various units and offices are loosely coupled with each other and with the central administration (Weick, 1976). Thus, units are only weakly related, information between them travels slowly and indirectly, and coordination is minimal. The notion of loose coupling helps explain the tension between centralized and decentralized decision making. Decisions are not coordinated across units, they happen independently. Information that may suggest particular and desired outcomes may not be shared widely, and decisions made in one place may be at odds with those made elsewhere. Longtime University of Chicago President Robert Hutchins's definition of a university serves as a pointed reminder of the nature of loose coupling in higher education: "The university is a collection of departments tied together by a common steam plant" (as cited in Birnbaum, 2004, p. 185).

The solution to address some of these institutional challenges often is to seek a tighter coupling. Administrators strive to coordinate, organize, and plan, which as management guru Mintzberg notes are all synonyms for control (2004). However, Weick argues that loosely coupled organizations have some important advantages over tightly coupled ones. First, loosely coupled systems are able to respond more sensitively to environmental changes. For example, new professional standards in accounting do not require a curricular overhaul throughout the institution, but only in one department. Second, loosely coupled organizations foster and sustain localized innovations, and, at the same time, quarantine poor adaptations. Good ideas that work well in one unit, such as requiring a service learning component in an undergraduate psychology program, do not require consensuses throughout the university, nor do they disrupt the academic curriculum of another department, such as engineering. And poor ideas do not spread easily throughout the institution. Third, loosely coupled organizations benefit from professional autonomy. For instance, central administrators do not need to be content experts in all disciplines. They can rely upon the expertise of department chairs and faculty leaders to make departmental decisions in ways that advance their disciplines. Finally, loosely coupled organizations can have lower costs because of less centralization and coordination. A large central bureaucracy is not required, allowing institutions more financial flexibility to invest in key core efforts (such as teaching and learning or scholarship). That said, loosely coupled organizations give up efficiency for lack of central coordination, do not easily disseminate needed innovation throughout the system, can be working at odds with other units, and are rarely responsive to the central core.

Decision Making via Garbage Cans

Academic decision making can seem unruly, and frequently resembles anarchy. Decisions are viewed as being made willy-nilly, attention seems to be given to trivial matters, key decision makers are easily distracted, and decisions that set out to address one concern end up resolving others that are unrelated. Cohen and March (1986) offer an explanation to these ongoing frustrations through the metaphor of a garbage can. Academic decisions, they argue, are confounded by the three key organizational conditions. First, colleges and universities pursue a set of inconsistent, ambiguous, and uncertain goals. For instance, institutions are concerned both with increased quality *and* widespread access; they seek the unfettered pursuit of knowledge *and* to leverage scientific breakthroughs for economic gain. Second, the ways in which they conduct their core functions, particularly teaching and learning, are unclear. Most faculty do not really know how students learn or understand the essential processes involved in creating civically minded students or globally competent citizens. Third, participation in organizational events is fluid as faculty and administrators choose among competing opportunities based upon their own preferences as to what is important. Although they are busy people, they cannot keep up with all of the demands on their time.

The effect of these organizational realities is that decisions depend upon the flow of (1) decision makers, (2) institutional problems, and (3) potential solutions that are present in the institution like three streams. Not all decisions are made by how most people like to envision decision making, that is, by (1) identifying all of the possible options, (2) speculating about the outcomes of each, and (3) making choices that maximize results. Instead, these three streams come together in a variety of metaphoric garbage cans throughout the institution where problems, solutions, and decision makers stick to each other rendering decisions. Thus, solutions are in search of problems as much as problems are in search of solutions, and decisions depend upon the mix in the garbage can at any particular time.

From this perspective, Cohen and March argue that decisions are made in one of three ways. They can be made by *resolution*, in which participants make a concerted effort to apply solutions to recognized problems. Decisions can be made by *flight*, when problems become attached to other unintended solutions or participants. For example, a suggested foreign language requirement can easily turn into conversations about faculty hiring or classroom space use, a different and potentially unrelated set of problems and solutions. Finally, decisions can be made by *oversight*. Key participants are too busy to participate in all decisions, so problems and solutions become coupled with little intention and involvement by key campus leaders.

The Other Impacts of Making Decisions

Understanding that governance leaves important marks on a campus beyond the decisions it makes does not ease frustrations with the process, but it can add some comfort. Birnbaum (1991) argues that academic decision bodies, such as senates, have both manifest and latent functions and it is not making decisions that matter as much as the other key institutional functions. Among his latent functions, he suggests that senates serve important symbolic roles. They confirm important professional values such as deference to faculty on academic matters and communicate faculty's professional obligations to those types of decisions. They acknowledge the idea of faculty prerogative on academic decisions and as a sign of cooperation between faculty and administrators. Senates signify and confirm status, particularly the right of faculty to have a voice in campus-wide matters, that puts them on common footing with administrators. Administrators have the organizational and legal prerogative to exert leadership, but senates validate the roles of others to exert their influence. Senates, as prestigious institutional bodies, provide a route for academic social mobility. They allow faculty a way out of the academic trenches onto the institution's center stage. Senates also serve as outlets for those with grievances to solicit potential support. Senates can serve as one of Cohen and March's garbage cans because they attract people and solutions, which may actually allow other decisions to be made more easily and intentionally elsewhere. Similarly, shared governance bodies work to limit the organizational impact of potentially disruptive ideas and temper administrative desire for change. Additionally, they can become the organization's deep freeze, keeping problematic or irrelevant problems from being acted upon. However, senates can also play an important role in sifting through an infinite number of institutional concerns to identify salient issues, even if they do not act on the issues themselves. Senates also become proving grounds for future administrators, as institutions look to their faculty ranks to fill important administrative vacancies. The routines of senates provide important rituals and outlets. As Birnbaum notes, "when one doesn't know that else to do, participating in senate debate can appear to be a contribution towards solutions" (p. 203). Finally, senates play important roles as scapegoats. When things go awry for unexplained reasons, the senate can easily take the blame, adding an important sense of causality to account for outcomes not easily explainable. From the perspective offered by Birnbaum, what may appear as organizational dysfunction on the surface actually contributes in important ways to the operation of the campus.

IMPLICATIONS FOR CAMPUS DECISION MAKERS

To create decision-making processes and structures that render effective decisions that match the demands of the day, and in ways that reflect the organizational realities of most colleges and universities, the most promising strategies likely will combine the straightforward with the unconventional. No simple solution exists to improve academic decision making. As Birnbaum writes, "Presidents, trustees, and others should be aware of thinking of better management as a panacea. Quick fixes and Gordian knot solutions have limited applications in all kinds of organizations and are particularly unlikely to be functional in colleges and universities" (1988, p. 202). And frequently, the suggested fix is to change the structure of governance or clarify roles of various participants, which is akin to the old saw of moving deck chairs on the *Titanic*. The problem typically lies much deeper and different tactics are called for. This is possibly why the AAUP's 1966 *Statement on Government* (AAUP, 1995) that articulates roles and responsibilities for different decision-making parties is not very effective in practice. What follows are some of the strategies leaders might consider.

First, decision makers should pay attention to process. Campus leaders must pay as much attention to the processes used to reach decisions as the content and potential impact of the decisions themselves. Any efforts to create new systems or to update existing capacities must not only address today's challenges but embody academic values and prize expertise. It is essential to balance the *what* of academic decision making with the *how* decisions are made. This simple challenge becomes troublesome when experienced leaders are confident in their abilities to effect change. It is their familiarity with their institutions and effecting change that tends to create a false confidence, leading people to pay too little attention to process (Eckel, Green, & Hill, 2001).

Second, legitimacy is paramount. Modifying existing decision-making processes to accommodate new challenges requires a careful and thorough understanding of the common definition of what constitutes a legitimate decision-making process. Key stakeholders, each often holding veto power from their varying authority bases, need to believe that they have opportunities to influence both process as well as outcomes. However, the components of a decision-making process that make it legitimate can greatly vary across institutions (Eckel, 2000). What may work well on one campus, on another may clearly violate expected norms. Leaders must have a fine-tuned eye to know what elements can be adjusted and what is sacred. If leaders adhere to processes that are legitimate, they shortcut unnecessary conversations about process (which can eventually derail important decisions) and instead allow those involved to focus on the decision at hand. Less distraction helps keep the material in the garbage can to a minimum.

Third, agree upon a common definition of "good governance." It is important that key stakeholders share a common understanding (implicit or explicit) of what constitutes good decision making. Oftentimes trouble occurs when different groups hold different implicit definitions. Thus, it is easy for one group to violate the expectations of another. One common example is the belief that only academic decisions can be made by campus senates. At some institutions this is true. However, others have developed legitimate ways that involve key faculty leaders in venues outside traditional senates structures, freeing the senate to address other issues of importance (Eckel, 2003).

Finding ways to reach a common understanding through action or discussion is important, but it is difficult in practice. An analogy is the difference between talking about being happily married and actually being happily married. What is easily agreed upon in conversation may be difficult to live up to daily. Some useful approaches (to governance, not marriage) include reviewing past decision-making processes (both good and bad) to cull key points; developing task forces to rethink governance processes, and do so through widely consultative and inclusive processes (such as campus-wide, mini-roundtable discussions); or developing and critiquing draft statements and white papers that explore key conceptions of academic decision making.

Fourth, appreciate that decisions are not always about rendering solutions. Much happens in colleges and universities that is equivocal and requires interpretation to make sense (Birnbaum, 1988). Is the closing of academic programs a sign of a university in decline or one that is shoring up its resources and mission on its way to excellence? Opportunities to make decisions can help an institution realize its preferences, determine its priorities, and understand its identity. A college or university may not know what it collectively thinks until it sees what it does (Weick, 1995). For example, discontinuing academic programs may help an institution clarify goals (i.e., to become a leading research university), make sense of confusing times (i.e., what does it mean to be a land-grant university in a state not committed to public higher education), and confirm shared institutional beliefs (i.e., to become a top-tier research university) (Eckel, 2003). Decisions to close programs bring key constituents together to build common perceptions of a turbulent environment, clarify values, sort out different understandings, and negotiate aspirations. Decisions provide opportunities for people to articulate what is happening in the world and in the organization and to explore why that is important, not just render decisions (March, 1994).

Finally, campus leaders need to have realistic expectations for academic decision making. Colleges and universities, and their decision-making processes, are human endeavors. They are susceptible to people's mistakes, oversights, conflicts, biases, passions, commitments, and preoccupations. The organizations in which decisions need to be made are complex, distracted, historic, obsessed, capricious, and fickle. The issues about which institutions must decide are often complicated and nuanced, with no clear solution, and usually, little precedent. Academic decision making must cope with these shortcomings and address the challenges of the times.

CONCLUSION: TOWARD EFFECTIVE DECISION MAKING

The points above suggest that creating effective academic decision-making processes is a complex and difficult undertaking. It is not uncommon to hear criticisms that it cannot keep up with the demands of a fast-paced, constantly changing environment and must be restructured to stay relevant. The shortcomings of academic decision making are that these processes are inclusive to a fault, result in decisions that can easily be vetoed by a small majority, and are often derailed or at least confused by other seemingly peripheral issues. Critics of academic decision making want efficient processes that lead to outcomes.

However, improving the efficiency of academic decision making may not increase its effectiveness. Efficiency and effectiveness are two organizational objectives that in campus governance more often may be at odds with one another than compatible, regardless of how often they are linked in everyday conversation. Efficiency is how smoothly functions are performed based on an input to output ratio; while effectiveness, on the other hand, is the extent to which the organization meets its goals (Pfeffer & Salancik, 1978). Organizations can be effective without being efficient, and they can be efficient without being effective. In a vote, we choose effectiveness. In fact, it might be the conditions that make colleges and universities effective—their decentralization, the reliance on faculty to deliver core functions and who pursue their own research agendas, and the ability of departments to pursue their own strategies—might be the same ones that make them inefficient. Colleges and universities invest for the long-term and often for the unknown. How many would have predicted a decade ago the national security need for Arabic languages or the economic demands of China?

What makes an academic decision effective? No simple answer exists. However, a starting point for that discussion might be that (1) the decision advances the well-being of the institution, (2) the decision reflects its culture and aspirations, and (3) the decision is implemented. This last point is the most important. Making and implementing decisions are two different and frequently unrelated processes.

To make decisions that are implemented, decision makers often have to make trade-offs between the optimal (or best) choice but an inactionable outcome and one that can gain the necessary commitment to be implemented. Brunsson (1982) argues that organizations face two decisions: one to chose the right thing, and two, to get things done. It is the latter that often requires irrationality because decision makers must take into consideration the various and competing motivations, understandings, preferences, and commitments of those involved in the decision process. Thus, higher education decisions that are able to be implemented may depend on what seems like overly abundant involvement and consultation, or may follow historic precedent even if those strategies no longer make pragmatic sense. The short of it on most campuses is that academic decisions that are implemented typically involve a range of key stakeholders whose different opinions and perspectives ensure that more options are considered and potential outcomes explored, and that decisions are discussed and debated more thoroughly than if they involved a limited number of people.

REFERENCES

American Association of University Professors. (1995). *Policy documents and reports* (8th ed.). Washington, DC: Author.

Anderson, E. L. (2002). *The new professoriate: Characteristics, contributions, and compensation*. Washington, DC: American Council on Education.

Baldridge, J. V. (1982). Shared governance: A fable about the lost Magic Kingdom. *Academe*, 68(1), 12–15.

Birnbaum, R. (1988). *How colleges work: The cybernetics of academic organization and leadership*. San Francisco: Jossey-Bass.

Birnbaum, R. (1991). The latent organizational functions of the academic senate: Why senates do not work but will not go away. In M. W. Peterson, E. E. Chaffee, & T. H. White (Eds.), *Organization and governance in higher education* (4th ed., pp. 195–207). Needham Heights, MA: Ginn Press.

Birnbaum, R. (2001). *Management fads in higher education: Where they come from, what they do, why they fail*. San Francisco: Jossey-Bass.

Birnbaum, R. (2004). *Speaking of higher education: The academic's book of quotations*. Westport CT: Praeger.

Bok, D. (2003). *Universities in the marketplace: The commercialization of higher education*. Princeton, NJ: Princeton University Press.

Brunsson, N. (1982). The irrationality of action and action rationality: Decisions, ideologies, and organizational actions. *Journal of Management Studies, 19*, 29–44.

Cohen, M. D., & March, J. G. (1986). *Leadership and ambiguity* (2nd ed.). Boston: Harvard Business School Press.

Eckel, P. D. (2000). The role of shared governance in institutional hard decisions: Enabler or antagonist? *Review of Higher Education, 24*, 15–39.

Eckel, P. D. (2003). *Changing course: Making the hard decisions to eliminate academic programs*. Westport, CT: Praeger.

Eckel, P., Green, M., & Hill, B. (2001). *On Change V: Riding the waves of change* (Occasional Paper No. 5). Washington, DC: American Council on Education.

Fairweather, J. (1996). *Faculty work and the public trust: Restoring the value of teaching and public service in American academic life*. Boston: Allyn & Bacon.

Hearn, J. C. (2003). *Diversifying campus revenue streams: Opportunities and risks*. Washington, DC: American Council on Education.

Kane, T. J., & Orszag, P. R. (2003, September). *Higher education spending: The role of Medicaid and the business cycle*. Washington, DC: The Brookings Institution. Retrieved September 2005, from http://www.brookings.edu/comm/policybriefs/pb124.pdf.

Kezar, A. (2001). Seeking a sense of balance: Academic governance in the 21st century. *Peer Review, 3*(3), 4–6.

Kirp, D. L. (2003). *Shakespeare, Einstein, and the bottom line*. Cambridge, MA: Harvard University Press.

March, J. G. (1994). *A primer on decision making: How decisions happen*. New York: Free Press.

Mintzberg, H. (1993). *Structures in fives: Designing effective organizations*. Englewood Cliffs, NJ: Prentice-Hall.

Mintzberg, H. (2004). *Managers not MBAs: A hard look at the soft practice of managing and management development*. San Francisco: Berrett-Koehler Publishers.

Newman, F., Couturier, L., & Scurry, J. (2004). *The future of higher education: Rhetoric, reality, and the risks of the market*. San Francisco: Jossey-Bass.

Pfeffer, J., & Salancik, G. R. (1978). *External control of organizations: A resource dependence perspective*. New York: Harper and Row.

Rosovsky, H. (1990). *The university: An owner's manual*. New York: Norton.

Slaugher, S., & Leslie, L. (1997). *Academic capitalism: Politics, policies, and the entrepreneurial university*. Baltimore: Johns Hopkins University Press.

State Higher Education Executive Officers. (2005). *Accountability for better results: A national imperative for higher education*. Denver, CO: Author. Retrieved October 2005 from http://www.sheeo.org/pubs/pubs_search.asp.

Weick, K. E. (1976). Educational organizations as loosely coupled systems. *Administrative Science Quarterly, 21*(1), 1–19.

Weick, K. E. (1995). *Sensemaking in organizations*. Thousand Oaks, CA: Sage Publications.

Weisbrod, B. A. (1998). The nonprofit mission and its financing: Growing links between nonprofits and the rest of the economy. In B. A. Weisbrod (Ed.), *To profit or not to profit: The commercial transformation of the nonprofit sector* (pp. 1–22). New York: Cambridge University Press.

Yudolf, M. (2002, January 11). Is the public research university dead? *The Chronicle of Higher Education* (p. B24).

CHAPTER

Centers, Institutes, and Academic Decision Making: Addressing "Suburban Sprawl" through Strategies for "Smart Growth"

William T. Mallon
Association of American Medical Colleges

Clark Kerr (1964) likened the modern research university to "a city of infinite variety" (p. 41). Kerr's analogy of the university as a city and its many parts remains an apt conceptual framework for the complexities and challenges of the modern research university—from the local flavor of academic departments akin to city neighborhoods, to the urban denizens we call faculty, to the complicated and sometimes strident academic governance and decision-making structures analogous to ward advisory boards and city councils.

I propose the extension of Kerr's metaphor of university as *city* to university as *metropolis* so as to include the burgeoning suburbs of modern academic life. The university's borders now reach far beyond its historical intertwined core functions of teaching, research, and service to include activities such as for-profit curricular ventures, strategic research alliances, distance education, and technology transfer. These peripheral functions and activities have developed as edge cities, if you will, complementary to (and, sometimes, competing with) the traditional academic core, with their own financial, physical, and human resources. The growth of these edge activities continues to push the university into far-flung frontiers where interactions with industry, corporate sponsors, and government and nongovernmental agencies can be common-place and can affect how decisions are made. Strategies for academic "smart growth," in these instances, can restrain unabated and potentially harmful sprawl.

In this chapter, I focus specifically on the growth of organized research units—that is, centers and institutes—in the suburbs of the university, the effects of that growth on the city center, and the implications for academic decision making. Research centers and institutes at universities are not new; they and their antecedents have been in existence as long as the research university itself (Friedman & Friedman, 1984; Rosenberg, 1976). The controversy over centers and institutes is not new either. As early as 1930, Abraham Flexner criticized the model of a research center as a "dubious" activity, "since it implies a possible separation of teaching and research" (p. 111). What is new, however, is the prominence and increasing importance of organized centers and institutes to the university's research mission, particularly in the biomedical fields. In an era of "big" bioscience, the higher education community increasingly views scientific research and the intellectual property it generates as keys to university prestige and prosperity, while political leaders covet science and technology advancement as an engine of regional socioeconomic development. Research centers and institutes seem to be an increasingly preferred mechanism for the advancement of these goals. Based on survey and case study research, this chapter explores how research centers and institutes—occupying a space in the suburbs of the university—influence governance and decision making throughout the university metropolis.

In this booming academic conurbation, traditional concepts of decision making (particularly the idea of shared governance) can seem frayed, even anachronistic. Scholars and commentators have hinted at these emerging governance challenges for some time. Kezar and Eckel (2004) considered how new kinds of academic workers (e.g., part-time and contract faculty) make shared governance more complex and problematic. Kennedy (1993) called for "new coalitions" of decision makers from both the institutional center and its periphery (p. 113). Bok (2003) cited the need for new decision-making models for entrepreneurial ventures. If the sprawl of research centers and institutes and other peripheral activities are contributing to tensions in academic governance and decision making, then faculty, administrators, and other leaders in higher education may wish to embark on strategies for "smart growth" to help ameliorate these concerns.

The thesis in this chapter is that major research universities have created centers and institutes (or have allowed centers and institutes to be created) to bolster research capacity as part of their strategy for growth, prominence, and economic development. Although many centers and institutes remain on the margins of academic life, some have accreted significant influence and power. In turn, this growth on the edge of the university creates a centrifugal force, shifting away from the traditional norms and pathways of academic decision making. These centers may very well challenge traditional notions of academic governance resting with the core faculty and departmental structure. As Kerr (1964) presciently observed, "much change takes place ... outside the 'veto groups' of the academic community.... The institute, in particular, has been as much the vehicle for innovation in recent years as the department has been the vault of tradition. Change comes more through spawning the new than reforming the old" (p. 102). This trend toward more research centers and institutes will continue rather than abate, given trends in funding and scholarship.

Figure 2.1
Expenditures for Academic R&D, 1975–2001

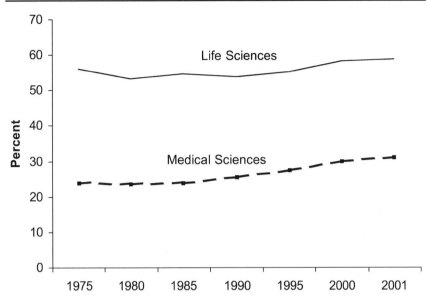

Source: Number Science Board, 2004, p. A5–11.

LIFE SCIENCES RESEARCH IN THE UNIVERSITY

This chapter focuses specifically on the role of centers and institutes in life science research in the modern university. Perhaps no other area in the modern academic metropolis has grown faster and larger over wider swaths than the academic research enterprise in the life sciences. Biomedical and health-related research has become a critical component of the academic research enterprise, nationally and internationally, for three main reasons: its dominant size in academic research, its potential for global impact, and its critical role in higher education's relationship to the international economy.

Size

In American higher education, health and medical research represents a vast commitment of financial and human resources. As displayed in Figure 2.1, 59 percent of all academic research and development expenditures went to the life sciences in 2001; medical sciences' share of all academic R&D increased from 23.8 percent to 31.1 percent from 1975 to 2001 (National Science Board, 2004). A small number of universities perform the bulk of academic life sciences research; 25 universities, composing just 5 percent of all higher education institutions that secured research grant funding from the National Institutes of Health (NIH) in fiscal year 2003, received 48 percent of that funding (NIH, 2004). Despite the apparent advantage of the largest universities to reap a disproportionate share of funding, competition for a piece of the life sciences pie remains fierce. States view bioscience as an engine of economic development, with a number of smaller regions—such as northern Kentucky/southern Ohio, Buffalo/Niagara, greater Oklahoma City, and central Indiana—attempting to develop biotech industries through academic collaborations (Blumenstyk, 2004).

Global Impact

A second reason why academic life sciences research has become so important is its potential to affect the human condition. Throughout the industrial and developing worlds, HIV/AIDS, cancer, communicable diseases, and chronic conditions damage national capacity and prematurely end human life. Through advances in areas such as genomics, proteomics, and molecular medicine, medical and life sciences research, more than any other area of academic research, has the potential to impact global society in the twenty-first century. But no other field of academic research is more fraught with complex challenges, such as ethical quandaries, financial constraints, and infrastructure problems.

Role in the International Economy

Third, biomedicine and biotechnology represent a prime example of higher education's emergence in an international knowledge economy. Research universities continue to exploit their basic science discoveries into commercially viable products. For example, the number of patents assigned to research universities increased 850 percent from 1980 to 1999; by the end of the twentieth century, more than 46 percent of those patents were biomedical in nature (Powell & Owen-Smith, 2002). The commercialization of the academic life sciences enterprise contributes to an international research economy—what Geiger (2004) calls "biocapitalism"—where the distinctions between academy and industry are increasingly blurred.

CENTERS AND INSTITUTES: PROMINENT OR PERIPHERAL?

I offer three propositions about the role of centers and institutes in the modern research university based on the following data: (1) a 2004 survey of the directors of 604 research centers and institutes located at major research universities and medical schools (Mallon & Bunton, 2005a, 2005b); (2) a 2005 survey of a random stratified sample of 285 basic science faculty with appointments at top-40 research-intensive medical schools (Bunton & Mallon, 2006); and (3) qualitative data from interviews with faculty, center directors, department chairs, and administrators at six research universities and their affiliated medical schools, conducted in 2004. The first proposition is that theories of growth, based on an extrapolation from the urban planning and economic development fields, explain why organized research units have gained prominence over time. Second, the majority of research centers remain in the margins of university decision making. Third, a smaller number of centers—what I will call "power centers"—have considerably more influence in university governance because of their access to formal and informal power and authority.

PROPOSITION #1: UNDERSTANDING THE GROWING SPRAWL OF RESEARCH INSTITUTES

Returning to the metaphor of metropolitan growth, every major (and even not-so-major) urban area in America is subject to sprawl—the development of subdivisions far from the city core, typically unplanned and uncoordinated, which results in changes and challenges to a region's infrastructure, governance, resources, and, ultimately, sustainability. Mieszkowski and Mills (1993) offer two theories for the sprawl of suburban development—individual choice and natural evolution—while Wassmer and Edwards (2005) suggest a theory of fiscalization of governance policies. Each of these theories can be applied to the sprawl of centers in the landscape of the university to help explain why centers and institutes have gained prominence and popularity.

Individual Choice

Mieszkowski and Mills's (1993) first theory for the cause of suburbanization can be characterized as an individual choice theory. Wishing to escape real or perceived social and fiscal problems that plague cities (such as low-quality schools, crime, high taxes, racial tensions, etc.), affluent individuals choose to move to the suburbs (thus, this theory is also called flight-from-blight). These individuals seek to associate with others of similar income levels, education, and race.

Applied to higher education, the individual choice theory would posit that the growth of centers and institutes can be explained by the actions of faculty members and administrators, individually and in groups, who create centers because of their desire to access additional resources (e.g., space, equipment, research and administrative staff) not available through academic departments, to reward or retain highly productive investigators with their own "home" outside the purview of the department chair, and to associate with other like-minded investigators.

Recent data on research centers support this theory of growth. First, centers act as both an intake valve and a funnel for financial resources. Research-oriented centers in a recent survey (Mallon & Bunton, 2005b) earned, on average, $5.7 million in annual financial support (the median funding amount was $2 million), 63 percent of which was derived from government grants and contracts.[1] In interviews, university administrators, faculty members, department chairs, and center directors often discussed this purpose and value of research centers:

- "We are an instrument for raising money. Departments don't always raise money very well. We can do that because we have a clear vision for what we want to do." (center director)

- "[I have proposed a number of institutes as part of a new strategic plan] to create a bold agenda that would capture public [interest] and allow us to raise funds." (dean)

- "Within the center we have a much larger opportunity to attract funds for equipment." (faculty member)

- "The idea of having institutes serves a purpose: raising funds." (department chair)

Second, university administrators have created centers to reward and retain highly productive faculty members who want independence in and recognition for their research programs. A dean at a large research university said, for example, "centers work here because they provide a certain amount of autonomy for faculty members who might not be able to get undivided or consistent support from the department chair." A dean at another institution noted that some centers "were created, candidly, to retain an individual—people who would say, 'I won't go to another university if you make me a center director.'"

Third, data indicate a "drawn-to-the-light" phenomenon whereby individuals choose to affiliate with research centers because of the stature of the "residents." In a national random sample of basic scientists at the top-40 research-intensive medical schools (as measured by NIH research grant funding), faculty members affiliated with research centers produced more peer-reviewed journal articles and were statistically more likely to be a principal investigator for external grants and contracts than those without center affiliations (Bunton & Mallon, 2006). If more productive faculty members affiliate with centers than those who are less productive, this situation may create a cycle of "flight from blight" where entrepreneurial and productive faculty are drawn to centers because they see their most successful peers and mentors doing the same. Moreover, the funding environment in the life sciences may increasingly reward interdisciplinary projects and approaches. The National Institutes of Health, for example, announced a "roadmap" initiative in 2003 to fund interdisciplinary research (Zerhouni, 2003) and private foundations have done the same (e.g., Doris Duke Charitable Foundation, 2003). Academic scientists, therefore, may increasingly choose to organize their work with highly desirable researchers from a variety of fields through the center structure.

Natural Evolution Model

The natural evolution model of Mieszowski and Mills (1993) suggests that suburban sprawl is a natural phenomenon, an inexorable result of higher incomes, transportation improvements, and housing development. Neighborhoods around a central business district develop first, but as land becomes saturated, new housing is built farther away from the city center. The most affluent groups move to these newer and more spacious areas, and the process then repeats itself: first-ring suburbs give way to developments farther out where land is more plentiful and less populated. We might call this theory the rippling of regional development.

This natural evolution model of suburbanization helps explain the development of research centers and institutes in the biomedical and life sciences. Historically, scientific disciplines were organized through academic departments "located at the heart of the university" (Rossi, 1964, p. 1160) and integral to the very nature of the academy (Abbott, 2002; Stahler & Tash, 1994). But as science continues to outgrow the epistemological departmental borders that the university has placed around it, the demand for interdisciplinary approaches to scientific research and training has pushed much cutting-edge work beyond these core departments. Just as the evolutionary model in urban development theory emphasizes an organic cycle of decay and redevelopment in cities, an evolutionary approach to the organizational structure of the university highlights the natural decline of some departments and the birth of other organizational forms. For example, in many medical schools, new departments such as neuroscience and genetics have been created while other existing departments, in areas such as anatomy, physiology, and pharmacology, have closed, consolidated, or merged (Mallon, Biebuyck & Jones, 2003).

The natural evolution theory of university centers would posit, therefore, that their creation is part of the inexorable natural growth of science from discipline- to interdisciplinary-driven investigations, which require structures to facilitate researchers from many fields. Extant data support this view. First, the number of centers and institutes has blossomed in the last 30 years (Figure 2.2). Second, centers and institutes in the life sciences are more interdisciplinary than in the past. A generation ago, Friedman and Friedman (1982) found less than one-third of centers in the biological sciences and only half of the centers in the medical sciences had interactions with more than one department; interactions with more than three departments were uncommon. In comparison, recent research (Mallon & Bunton, 2005b) has shown that centers and institutes in 2004 involved faculty from a greater number of departments (mean = 4.89, median = 4). Only 15 percent of centers involved faculty from a single department in 2004; 70 percent of centers include faculty representing three or more departments (Table 2.1). In the Friedmans' 1982 study, 23 percent of medical science centers and 24 percent of biological science centers agreed that their approach to work could be characterized as interdisciplinary.[2] Mallon and Bunton (2005b) found, however, that modern research centers in the biomedical and health-related fields embrace more interdisciplinary approaches to their work than those centers in the 1980s. Forty-two percent of the research centers in the 2004 study indicated that their approach to research was interdisciplinary, with an additional 39 percent indicating multidisciplinary, 7 percent unidisciplinary, and 12 percent some combination of the categories—a substantial increase in the percentage of centers embracing interdisciplinary approaches to their activities.

Through the creation of organized research centers, universities appear to be responding to the demands of science for increased interaction among investigators from many fields. In other words, universities are naturally adapting and

Figure 2.2
Number of Research Centers as Reported in the *Research Centers Directory*

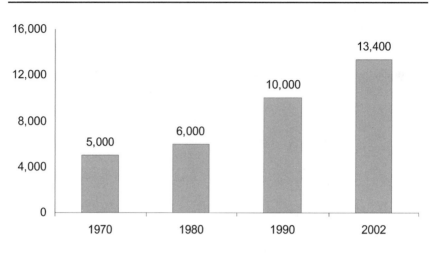

Table 2.1
Comparison of Interdisciplinarity and Faculty Involvement in Centers, 1982 and 2005

	Friedman & Friedman (1982)		Mallon & Bunton (2005b)
	Medical Sciences	Biological Sciences	
Approach to research:			
Interdisciplinary*	20%	24%	42%
Multidisciplinary*	60%	58%	39%
Unidisciplinary*	20%	18%	7%
Some combination of categories	0%	1%	12%
Departments represented in work:			
One department	50%	69%	15%
3 departments or more	38%	19%	70%

* See note 2 for explanation of definitions.

evolving in response to science itself. The natural evolution theory of growth would suggest that centers and institutes have rapidly populated the research landscape in higher education because they transcend disciplinary affiliations and can often quickly respond to new research directions.

Fiscalization Theory

Wassmer and Edwards (2005) offer a third theory about the development of sprawl. The fiscalization theory stipulates that outlying locales are more likely to encourage the development of unpopulated land if government policy makes it economically beneficial to do so. The more likely that fiscal considerations drive decisions about land use, the more likely the region will suffer from sprawl. For example, if state policy allows local governments to retain sales tax, these localities will encourage retail development (and the concomitant housing development to support it) to add tax revenues to their coffers.

Transferred to the expanding boundaries of the research university, the fiscalization theory posits that if university policies allow local entities (i.e., centers and institutes) to benefit economically, then entrepreneurial growth in the suburbs of the university will blossom. The most likely scenario under which this type of growth would occur is when the university permits a portion of indirect costs recovered from sponsored research grants to be retained by the center or institute. A university's fiscal policy may also encourage the creation of centers when the institution itself offers start-up seed funding for new research collaborations. The provost's office at the University of North Carolina, Chapel Hill, for example, can offer initial funds of $50,000–60,000 per year to seed innovative research centers, with the expectation that they will become self-sustaining through extramural grant support. The University of Alabama, Birmingham, has a similar program that provides $55,000 in annual institutional funding to new research collaborations for a two-year cycle. To achieve buy-in throughout the institution, the directors of these centers must raise 30 percent of their budgets from individual school deans.

Geiger (2004) states that entrepreneurial universities—those that "tend to regard the expansion of their research portfolio as an end in itself … that need not be justified by links with instruction"—may use centers and institutes, research faculty, and indirect cost recovery as a means of bolstering the research enterprise (p. 70). Universities that allow indirect costs to be retained by the research unit provide an important incentive in spurring additional research activities and projects. The University of Michigan is a case in point of how fiscal policy prompts growth. With $5 to $10 million in annual funding in the 1990s from the university to seed and promote new research, Michigan had more than 160 research centers by 2000, more than half of which were created in the previous decade (Geiger, 2004, p. 163).

These three theories of growth of centers and institutes are complementary, not competing, and together offer rich explanations for the development of the sprawling life sciences infrastructure in American research universities. The question that remains is to what extent these entities affect the traditional academic core. Does the development of the suburbs make a difference to the city center? The next two propositions assert that the answer is both "no" and "yes."

PROPOSITION #2: MOST CENTERS REMAIN IN THE MARGINS

Many, if not most, research centers and institutes remain in the outer reaches of the university's power structure and process. Previous scholarship has noted that centers are "at" the university but not "of" it (Ikenberry & Friedman, 1972). That is, centers operate at the periphery of the university, not at the core. Although centers serve important purposes, traditional orthodoxy instructs that they "will never replace academic departments in terms of ... organizational primacy" (Stahler & Tash, 1994, p. 552).

More recently, however, some commentators have expressed concern about the preeminent role of the academic department (Fischman, 1998; Galbreath, 2004; Ibrahim, et al., 2003), even suggesting that the departmental structure in the basic biological sciences is an outdated concept (Moses, Their, & Matheson, 2005). As centers and institutes grow, it has been argued, they may challenge the traditional role of departments by impinging on departmental integrity, usurping power and influence, and creating divided faculty loyalties. Do centers pose a threat to the organizational integrity of the university? Telling indicators of centers assuming status on par with departments would be their ability to appoint faculty and pay faculty salaries. Traditionally, academic departments have maintained the sole prerogative to appoint faculty and serve as the locus of faculty compensation. Centers and institutes with authority in one or both of these areas would indicate an important shift in university organization and structure.

But this shift has not occurred. Mallon and Bunton (2005b) found that most centers do not have the prerogative to directly appoint faculty: 78 percent had no faculty with primary center appointments, a finding similar to Ikenberry and Friedman's 1972 study, in which two-thirds of centers did not have appointment authority. Sixty-three percent of faculty members received no salary support from the centers with which they were affiliated; 27 percent of faculty received partial salary support, and only 10 percent of center-affiliated faculty received full salary support (Mallon & Bunton, 2005b). These data suggest that most centers and institutes have not assumed primacy in the life of faculty members, and thus, the academy, because they do not have power over two critical aspects of faculty work life—appointment authority and compensation. Other data support this view. In a 2005 faculty survey, 69 percent of basic science faculty with center affiliations indicated that their sense of identity as a faculty member was grounded in the department that held their primary appointment; 16 percent stated that they identified equally with center and department, and only 15 percent identified primarily with the center (Bunton & Mallon, 2006).

The department remains strong not only because of its functional roles in key activities such as appointment and promotion authority, but also because it is the locus of status and scholarly legitimacy. One provost noted, "Faculty gain their legitimacy, gain their peer approval, primarily through their departments." Faculty also share this view. One key reason is that the department acts as a rich source for academic mentoring, especially for junior faculty. An associate dean

Figure 2.3
Opinions of Center Directors

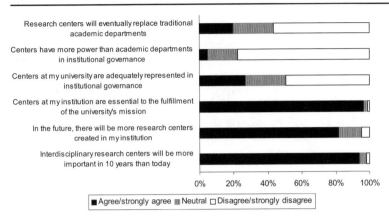

commented, "Departments provide the greatest security and the best opportunity for the mentoring of the individual along a particular career path." A department chair observed, "Faculty who were physically separated from their departments and were not getting the type of mentoring from the discipline-specific people in their department ... did not succeed."

Another indicator of how much status and authority centers and institutes enjoy is their placement in the structure of the university. Mallon and Bunton (2005b) found that the vast majority of research centers and institutes were not integrated at high levels of the university hierarchy. A plurality of centers (46 percent) reported to the medical school dean or graduate school dean; 34 percent reported to an associate dean, department chair, or another center director. From an organizational structure perspective (Bolman and Deal, 1997), these reporting relationships imply that more than one-third of centers have less status than, and only about one-half have similar status as, academic departments.[3]

Even if most centers do not have the personnel or structural authority to change the city-suburb dynamic, might they be able to do so politically? Most center directors did not believe their units occupy a place near the core of the university's decision making and power. Fifty-seven percent of center and institute directors disagreed or strongly disagreed with the idea that centers and institutes will eventually replace traditional departments; another 23 percent were neutral (Figure 2.3). More than three-quarters of the directors did not believe that centers and institutes had more power than academic departments in institutional governance, and 49 percent of directors did not believe that centers and institutes are adequately represented in institutional governance; another 24 percent were neutral. These results indicate that, on average, directors of biomedical centers and institutes believe that their units remain in the margins of institutional power, influence, and decision making. Administrators echo this idea as well. A chancellor likened departments and centers to the solar system. "If you think of the universe system as an analogy, departments and schools are the planets, but the centers are these shooting stars exploding and moving in a fast speed, not connected to the gravitation of the sun necessarily, but on their own."

Even if centers remain outside traditional power and decision-making struc-tures, they are important to the mission of the university, and many believe their role will continue to grow. The majority of directors believe that centers at their institution are essential to the fulfillment of the university's mission (97 percent agreed or strongly agreed); more than 80 percent agreed or strongly agreed that there will be more centers created at their institutions in the future; and 94 per-cent agreed or strongly agreed that interdisciplinary research centers will be more important in 10 years than they are today (Mallon & Bunton, 2005b).

Taken together, these data suggest that center directors believe their units have a strong and important presence in the life of the university but not in its power and decision-making structures. The vast majority of research centers have little direct influence on the governance of the university metropolis.

PROPOSITION #3: POWER CENTERS ARE CENTRAL

Not all centers, however, are relegated to inconsequential organizational roles. A contingent of centers and institutes, what I will call Power Cen-ters, have gained influence and power by dint of their considerable reach and resources. These research centers report to a university president, provost or vice president, independent board of trustees, or multicollege committee; have larger staffs; and secure more overall funding than other centers (Figure 2.4). These resources have led some Power Center directors to think of their units more boldly than most centers directors do. For example, a greater pro-portion of Power Center directors believe that research centers will eventually replace traditional academic departments than do those reporting to an asso-ciate dean, department chair, or another director (27 percent compared to 17 percent).

Why are Power Centers, in fact, powerful? Data from interviews with faculty and administrators at six major research universities provide insight to the rea-sons. First, these center directors are consulted by academic leaders on matters of importance and can shape decision outcomes. One center director explained: "I interact with the various deans [about] where they're heading and what they're doing, what kind of decisions they're making, what kind of hires should be done.... I'm on various groups that the vice chancellor, chancellor, and provost put together." Second, they are able to secure institutional resources quite readily, often in informal ways that are not afforded to many others in the academic com-munity. Said one Power Center director, "The provost's door is always open. I've been over there several times, saying 'More money, please,' and he's been great about that." Third, their position in the university gives them constant access to decision makers outside traditional channels:

Figure 2.4
Average Center Funding and Number of Staff, by Reporting Relationship

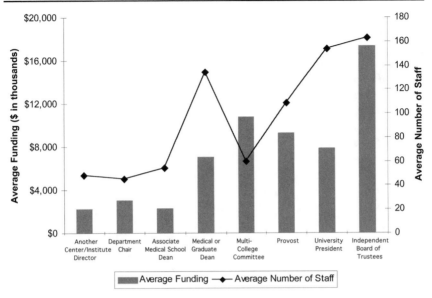

Administrator: The center directors who report to the vice chancellor have a lot of influence on him because they meet with him, lay out their agenda, and he reckons with it. I know he listens to them very carefully and does things in response to what they said, but it's not formal—it's outside the governance or policy-making system.

Interviewer: They have informal influence?

Administrator: Yes. One center that just landed a $70 million grant that has huge influence. Many of the faculty associated with that center have huge influence. The Vice Chancellor would not be long for this world if he was not listening to the needs of those centers.

Finally, while many of these Power Centers do not hold seats in the typical governance bodies of an institution, their directors do not feel the need to, given their other means to connect to prominent decision makers. One center director dismissed the need to partake in formal governance mechanisms because, "we have the ear of the President and we've got a lot of attention from the deans, so that's working just fine now."

Most research centers and institutes, to be sure, do not have such perks and privileges. This small group, however, operates outside traditional governance and decision-making processes, with ready, and even immediate, access to those individuals who control both purse and policy.

STRATEGIES FOR SMART GROWTH

Despite many centers' existence on the margins of institutional influence, they remain important mechanisms for supporting and sustaining the research enterprise. If the reader accepts the three propositions—that research centers and institutes continue to sprawl, that most centers remain in the margins, and that a smaller group of centers are prominent and powerful—the question then becomes how can and should the university manage and govern in this milieu. Let us again turn to lessons from the field of urban and regional planning, where many argue that the antidote for suburban sprawl is "smart growth."

Smart growth is a policy perspective that seeks to accommodate, rather than prohibit, growth (Haines, 2003). The literature from regional planning and design, geography, and environmental studies notes several tools to manage growth and development in metropolitan areas, including

- zoning ordinances and growth boundaries, both of which permit or prohibit land development in certain areas or under certain conditions;
- mixed-use development, in which different types of development are combined into one project;
- comprehensive planning, which is based on overall, not jurisdictional, boundaries;
- smart growth incentives, which encourage policies that promote sustainable growth; and
- "New Urbanism," a movement that seeks to rebuild and sustain cities.

I want to transfer the tools of smart growth in regional planning to the management and governance of research universities, reminding the reader that smart growth not only focuses on managing growth in the suburbs, but also seeks to maintain the vibrancy and sustainability of cities.

Zoning and Regulatory Strategies

In regional development, tools such as zoning and growth boundaries aim to regulate land use. For decades, commentators have suggested similar ideas for higher education: that the university should regulate, and even prohibit, the creation and development of centers and institutes (Dressel, Johnson, & Marcus, 1969; Friedman & Friedman, 1984; Stahler & Tash, 1994). Strict controls, however, would be detrimental to the overall health of the academic research enterprise, given the important and integral roles that centers and institutes play. As Geiger (1990) notes, organized research units "have powerfully abetted the operations of precisely those factors that are usually credited with underpinning the research prowess of American universities" (p. 16). Other tools of smart growth, discussed below, would be more effective in the academic setting.

Comprehensive Planning

Comprehensive regional planning is decision making on a regional level rather than a municipal level, in which city and surrounding counties and towns collaborate to serve the common good rather than focus solely on individual juris-dictional needs. Cities and suburbs will fight over limited resources without a clear comprehensive policy that recognizes that the health of the metropolis depends on the continued vibrancy of both areas. In the academic context, tensions arise between centers and departments over the allocation of financial, human, and physical resources. A strategy for this problem is mechanisms to allocate resources that benefit both interested parties. Indirect costs from sponsored grant funding, for example, may be allocated to both center and department based on a formula that takes into consideration the entity providing the investigator's space, grants administration, and faculty appointment. At the University of North Carolina, Chapel Hill, School of Medicine, for example, 50 percent of indirect costs returned to the faculty-level administrative unit goes to the entity (department or center) providing the investigator's space, 25 percent to whichever unit (department or center) administers the grant, and 25 percent to the unit that controls the faculty appointment (in every case, a department, not a center). Whatever the formula, these allocations should be in the public domain and consistently applied across the institution—not decided through private, closed-doors deals.

Smart Growth Incentives

Incentives in regional planning encourage development in some areas and dis-courage it in others. For example, state funding might be offered to communities that develop and support a robust public transportation system, or tax breaks may be offered to people who commute by bus or rail. Similarly, universities can offer peer-reviewed seed funding to generate new research centers and collaborations. For example, as described earlier, the University of Alabama, Birmingham, offers a competitive, refereed application process to support several new interdisciplin-ary research centers for a two-year cycle, with the intent that the most successful and promising ventures will become ongoing and self-sufficient through external grant funding. The key to this type of incentive is the time-honored traditions of peer-review and competition to ensure credibility, institutional integrity, and scientific rigor. A program of competitive seed funding for new centers awarded through scientific peer-review can spur new research areas, motivate entrepre-neurial investigators, and maintain the adaptive nature of research centers, all while promoting intellectual rigor and institutional accountability.

Mixed-Use Development

A fourth smart growth strategy is mixed-use development, in which one project is required to incorporate different development uses. For example, a new suburban housing development may be required to have facilities for retail stores such as groceries, dry cleaners, and restaurants all within walking distance. Similarly, higher education institutions may determine that certain types of organized research units—say, those that are designated as "university-level" institutes—should incorporate the missions of research, teaching, and service. The rationale behind this strategy is that some centers and institutes are so large, prominent, and visible that they ought to be required not only to generate new knowledge but also to contribute to the teaching and service aspects of the academy. Pennsylvania State University College of Medicine, for example, proposed a model that differentiates "institutes" from "centers" and other types of units based on the ways they contribute to the academic missions:

> Institutes, centers, consortia, and programs will be defined and differentiated based on the degree of integration of the four core missions of patient care, research, education, and community outreach. Defined … as the most comprehensive entity and the one with the highest level of institutional support, an institute must incorporate *all four* missions. A center is generally more limited in scope and is likely to receive relatively less institutional support; it would be required to involve *at least two* of the four core missions. A consortium or program must encompass emphasis in *at least one* of the four missions.

"New Urbanism": Renewing the Core

A fifth and final strategy for academic smart growth is based on the idea of "New Urbanism" in the urban planning field, a movement that rebuilds urban communities with pedestrian friendly neighborhoods, interactive meeting and gathering spaces, and nearby retail stores and services—all aimed to make cities more livable and sustainable. This idea, translated to academe, emphasizes an approach in which faculty and administrators attend to the future of disciplines and departments in addition to research centers and institutes. It recognizes that the academic core, represented by departments, goes through natural life cycles of growth and decline. Faculty and administrators routinely should revisit these disciplinary habitats for opportunities for renewal and revitalization. Disciplines, and the departments through which they are structured, are human creations and reflect people's habits and assumptions, which can evolve and even become outdated; they are no more a fixed order in nature than are city neighborhoods. Departments are born and mature; they can spawn new fields or can be supplanted by emerging disciplines, as demonstrated by the reorganization of many anatomy departments and the creation of neuroscience and genetics departments (Mallon, Biebuyck, & Jones, 2003). The review and renewal or revitalization of core departments should be a key strategy for academic smart growth, to ensure that organizational structure enhances rather than impedes the progress of science.

IMPLICATIONS FOR ACADEMIC DECISION MAKING

Universities have increasingly used research centers and institutes as a way of organizing and promoting their life sciences research enterprise. As the data in this chapter show, many of these centers may not have a significant impact on the governance of the university, but others do. The continued growth of the "biocapitalism" enterprise in universities and the concomitant growth of centers and institutes, particularly those I identify as Power Centers, have two paradoxical implications for decision making across the academic metropolis: as governance becomes more oligarchical, it also becomes more pluralistic.

On the one hand, academic decision making becomes more oligarchical as influence devolves from the collective faculty to the elite individual. Research "rainmakers" and faculty entrepreneurs in biocapitalism fields have the potential to impact important decisions about direction of effort, allocation of resources, and other areas than do most faculty through traditional governing processes. A handful of highly productive faculty investigators in every university account for a disproportionate amount of research funding. Ohio State University, for example, reported that just six researchers brought in one-quarter of all extramural research funds netted by the OSU medical school in fiscal year 2004—a total of $41 million (Ohio State University College of Medicine, 2005). These types of faculty members, in turn, can acquire high levels of influence that run parallel to traditional academic decision-making structures. My supposition is that these types of individual faculty members have much greater influence on the strategic direction of the enterprise than does the collective faculty.

Second, governance becomes more oligarchical as some organized research centers, particularly Power Centers, have increasing influence within the university to a greater degree than faculty governing groups and committees. Comprehensive cancer centers are a prime example. The National Cancer Institute, part of the National Institutes of Health, dictates that university-based comprehensive cancer centers have formal authority in the university hierarchy that supercedes academic departments. The NCI requirements state that "the organizational status of the cancer center and authority of the center director" must be "comparable or superior to that of departments and department chairs" (NCI, 2004, p. 13). Furthermore, universities are required to ensure that the center director has "at a minimum, joint control (for example, with a department chair) of recruitments of individuals who are to be members of the cancer center" as well as "full or shared control" over space and equipment and "control over philanthropic funds" (NCI, 2004, p. 13). These types of centers continue to challenge traditional notions of academic governance resting with the core faculty and departmental structure.

On the other hand, as governance and decision making become consolidated in an elite group of individual faculty members and administrators, it also becomes, paradoxically, more pluralistic. An influx of part-timers, non–tenure-track and contract faculty, and research scientists continue to secure pathways to represent their interests in an increasingly pluralistic system of campus governance. Mallon and Bunton (2005a) found, for example, that many nonfaculty professional research staff affiliated with centers and institutes had access to perquisites once tightly held only by tenured faculty: 59 percent could be principal investigators, 52 percent could participate in school- or university-level policy committees, and 32 percent could participate in the academic senate. In effect, centers are adding new players into the familiar system. With more voices in academic decision making, the dominance of traditional faculty, particularly the faculty senate, wanes. Although the entrepreneurial individual investigator and the once-disenfranchised academic staff may benefit from these trends, the outcome of this paradox for traditional faculty conclaves is a diluted voice in decisions.

Motivated by the market, prodded by external patrons, responding to demands of academic stars, the university will continue to build the organizational periphery. The long-term impact on the traditional neighborhoods of academic governance, therefore, depends upon balanced investment and development of the university metropolis.

NOTES

I would like to thank Sarah Bunton for her invaluable assistance in the preparation of this chapter. The data in the chapter are drawn from our combined work (Mallon & Bunton, 2005a and 2005b and Bunton & Mallon, 2006).

1. The remaining sources of funding were as follows: Universities themselves supplied 13 percent of funds, followed by private foundations (8 percent), industry/corporate funding (5 percent), center endowment (4 percent), other resources (3 percent), patient care services (2 percent), and direct state funds (2 percent).

2. Friedman and Friedman adopted the framework initially offered by Alpert (1969), which defined an interdisciplinary approach as faculty from different disciplines working together on the same project; multidisciplinary as faculty from different disciplines working independently on different aspects of a project; and unidisciplinary as faculty from a single discipline working together, using consultants from other disciplines as needed. Mallon and Bunton (2005b) used the same definitions for comparative purposes.

3. Another 15 percent of centers reported to the university president or chancellor, provost, independent board of trustees, or multicollege committee. These centers may be entities of considerable prestige because reporting to one of these individuals or groups may provide access to important campus decision makers. This subset of centers is explored in greater depth in proposition #3.

REFERENCES

Abbott, A. (2002). The disciplines of the future. In S. Brint (Ed.), *The future of the city of intellect: The changing American university* (pp. 205–230). Stanford, CA: Stanford University Press.

Alpert, D. (1969, December). *The role and structure of interdisciplinary and multidisciplinary research centers*. Paper presented at the annual meeting of the Council of Graduate Schools in the United States, Washington, DC. (ERIC Document Reproduction Service No. ED035363)

Blumenstyk, G. (2004, November 26). In the life sciences, a sprouting competition. *The Chronicle of Higher Education*, pp. A23–26.

Bok, D. (2003). *Universities in the marketplace: The commercialization of higher education.* Princeton, NJ: Princeton University Press.

Bolman, L.G., & Deal, T. E. (1997). *Reframing organizations.* San Francisco: Jossey-Bass.

Bunton, S .A., & Mallon, W.T. (2006). The impact of centers and institutes on faculty life: Findings from a study of basic science and internal medicine faculty at research-intensive medical schools. *Academic Medicine, 80,* 725–732.

Doris Duke Charitable Foundation (2005). Clinical interfaces award program. Retrieved May 1, 2005, from http://www.ddcf.org/page.asp?pageid=299.

Dressel, P. L., Johnson, F. C., & Marcus, P. M. (1969, July-August). The proliferating institutes. *Change, 21*–24.

Fischman, D. A. (1998, June). What role will chairs of discipline-based subjects play in the evolving medical school of the future? *FASEB Journal, 12,* 621–624.

Flexner, A. (1930). *Universities: American, English, German.* New York: Oxford University Press.

Friedman R. S., & Friedman, R. C. (1982, June). *The role of university organized research units in academic science.* University Park: Pennsylvania State University, Center for the Study of Higher Education. (NTIS No. PB82–253394)

Friedman R. S., & Friedman, R. C. (1984, Winter). Managing the organized research unit. *Educational Record, 65,* 27–30.

Galbreath, A. D. (2004, Winter). The center of the issue: Structure of centers and institutes within academic medicine. *Alliance for Academic Internal Medicine Insight.* Retrieved April 27, 2006, from http://www.im.org/AAIM/Pubs/Insight/Winter2004/page6.pdf.

Geiger, R. L. (1990, January/February). Organized research units—their role in the development of university research. *Journal of Higher Education, 61,* 1–19.

Geiger, R. L. (2004). *Knowledge and money: Research universities and the paradox of the marketplace.* Stanford, CA: Stanford University Press.

Haines, A.L. (2003, Spring). Smart growth: Solution to sprawl? *The Land Use Tracker.* Retrieved April 27, 2006, from http://www.uwsp.edu/cnr/landcenter/tracker/spring2003/SmartGrowth.html.

Ibrahim, T., O'Connell, J. B., LaRusso, N. F., Meyers, F. J., & Crist, T. B. (2003). Centers, institutes, and the future of the clinical department: Part 1. *American Journal of Medicine, 115,* 337–341.

Ikenberry, S. O., & Friedman, R. C. (1972). *Beyond academic departments.* San Francisco: Jossey-Bass.

Kennedy, D. (1993). Making choices in the research university. In J. R. Cole, E. G. Barger, & S. R. Graubard (Eds.), *The research university in a time of discontent* (pp. 85–114). Baltimore: Johns Hopkins University Press.

Kerr, C. (1964). *The uses of the university.* Cambridge, MA: Harvard University Press.

Kezar, A., & Eckel, P. (2004, July/August). Meeting today's governance challenges: A synthesis of the literature and examination of a future agenda for scholarship. *Journal of Higher Education, 75,* 371–399.

Mallon, W. T., Biebuyck, J. F, & Jones, R. F. (2003, March). The reorganization of basic science departments in U.S. medical schools, 1980–1999. *Academic Medicine, 78,* 302–306.

Mallon, W. T., & Bunton, S. A. (2005a). *Characteristics of research centers and institutes at U.S. medical schools and universities.* Washington, DC: Association of American Medical Colleges.

Mallon, W. T., & Bunton, S. A. (2005b). Research centers and institutes at U.S. medical schools: A descriptive analysis. *Academic Medicine, 80,* 1005–1011.

Mieszkowski, P., & E. S. Mills. (1993, Summer). The causes of metropolitan suburbanization. *Journal of Economic Perspectives, 7,* 135–147.

Moses, H., Their, S. O., & Matheson, D. H. (2005, March 23/30). Why have academic medical centers survived? *Journal of the American Medical Association, 293,* 1495–1500.

National Cancer Institute (2004, September). *The Cancer Centers Branch of the National Cancer Institute policies and guidelines relating to the Cancer Center Support Grant.* Bethesda, MD: Author. Retrieved May 1, 2005, from http://www3.cancer.gov/cancercenters/download/CCSG_Guide12_04.pdf.

National Institutes of Health (2004). *Extramural data and award trends.* Retrieved May 1, 2005, from http://grants1.nih.gov/grants/award/award.htm.

National Science Board (2004). *Science and engineering indicators 2004.* Arlington, VA: National Science Foundation. (NSB 04–1 and 04–1A)

Ohio State University College of Medicine (2005, January 27). Countdown to the top tier in 2008 means continuing upward climb. *The Ohio State University College of Medicine and Public Health News.* Retrieved April 27, 2006, from http://medicine.osu.edu/news/article.cfm?ID=1912.

Powell, W. W., & Owen-Smith, J. (2002). The new world of knowledge production in the life sciences. In S. Brint (Ed.), *The future of the city of intellect: The changing American university* (pp. 107–130). Stanford, CA: Stanford University Press.

Rosenberg, C. E. (1976). Science, technology, and economic growth: The case of the agricultural experiment station scientist, 1875–1914. In *No other gods: On science and American social thought* (pp. 153–172). Baltimore: Johns Hopkins University Press.

Rossi, P. H. (1964, Fall). Researchers, scholars, and policy makers: The politics of large scale research. *Daedalus, 93,* 1142–1167.

Stahler, G. J., & Tash, W. R. (1994). Centers and institutes in the research university: Issues, problems, and prospects. *Journal of Higher Education, 65,* 540–554.

Wassmer, R. W., & Edwards, D. (2005). *Causes of urban sprawl (decentralization) in the United States: Natural evolution, flight from blight, and the fiscalization of land use.* Paper prepared for the 2004 National Tax Association Conference, Minneapolis, MN. Retrieved April 27, 2006, from http://www.csus.edu/indiv/w/Wassmerr/WassmerEdwardsCausesSprawl.pdf.

Zerhouni, E. (2003, October 3). The NIH roadmap. *Science, 302,* 63–72.

CHAPTER

Charging into the Market: Governance Challenges Created by the Fit and Fitness of Commercial Activities

Jared Bleak
Duke University

Entrepreneurial activity in higher education has mushroomed in the last decade. In the gold rush fever of the late 1990s, education became the new Sutter's Mill with educational "prospectors" dreaming of finding their fortunes online and in the classroom. Where once the academy was risk-averse, "wary of corporate largesse," and content to seclude itself from market forces, it has now become an "eager co-capitalist, embracing market values as never before" (Press & Washburn, 2000, p. 41).

The charge into the market by colleges and universities in search of new revenue streams, increased enrollments, greater prestige, and amplified visibility for their "brand names" became common practice in the late 1990s and the early twenty-first century. Marketing and promotional campaigns to increase revenues are now commonplace. For example, 14 public universities contracted with the Collegiate Licensing Corporation and the Starter athletic apparel company to display their logos on a NASCAR series race car, guaranteeing each institution royalty income from sales of related NASCAR promotional items, an up-front payment for participating, and the opportunity to have their logo paraded before up to 90,000 fans on race day (Frye, 2001). Some universities sell to the highest bidder the naming rights to their sports arenas—for example, Comcast Center at the University of Maryland at College Park and Save Mart Center at California State University at Fresno—while others have even joined the cola wars by signing lucrative contracts that guarantee soft drink companies exclusive "pouring rights" on their campuses (Suggs, 2000; Van Der Werf, 1999).

Commercialization may be most dramatic in athletics, with multimillion-dollar coaching contracts, ever-lengthening seasons, and game schedules created to accommodate television, regardless of students' academic schedules. Case in point—for two straight seasons, the University of Oregon has rented high-priced space on a Manhattan skyscraper hoping to put its football program "on the national map" (Rhoden, 2002). Said one university official explaining the institution's rationale, "If you're not located in a media center, you go to the center." In 2001, Oregon spent $250,000 on a banner near Madison Square Garden, and in 2002, the price tag rose to $300,000 for a huge banner overlooking Times Square, beckoning passersby to ogle the university's star player and urging them to watch the team on television (Wojnarowski, 2002).

Following the example of the airlines, health clubs, and other industries that manage load factors and demand, universities offer students discounts on afternoon courses, hoping to relieve some of the strain on resources during the more popular morning hours (Farrell, 2002). And, in an effort to keep alumni and students' disposable income on campus and create an additional source of revenue, many universities have opened convenience stores and purchased nearby hotels. Not surprisingly, these market-oriented activities have not been universally admired. Said one skeptic, "A university's core mission is not operating a hotel" (June, 2002).

THE FOR-PROFIT SUBSIDIARY

One unconventional strategy colleges and universities are pursuing to increase their market-oriented activities is through the development of for-profit companies (particularly subsidiaries of the parent university or college). This approach is an extreme example of revenue-generating strategies. The availability of private capital for postsecondary education and the success of for-profit colleges and universities, such as the University of Phoenix, motivated nonprofit universities to explore the viability of these for-profit subsidiaries (Goldstein, 2000; Ruch, 2001). These companies were enticing because they were considered more nimble, entrepreneurial, and adaptable than their comparatively staid nonprofit parents (Goldstein, 2000; Kwartler, 2000). Not surprisingly, in governing these new entities, speed in decision making and a strategic market orientation—qualities that are often foreign to the traditional academy—were considered the sine qua non for success (Goldstein, 2000; Kwartler, 2000).

Although university owned for-profit subsidiaries once captured headlines for their anticipated gains and even more headlines for their fall (Columbia's Fathom is a case in point), they still quietly exist, and many believe their promise remains (Bleak, 2005; Blum, 2002; Carlson, 2000b).

These subsidiaries have both their supporters and detractors, and have generated their own degree of controversy. Although some contend that the academy must adapt to new market-driven realities, others argue that these for-profit organizations are inimical to the core values of higher education: shared governance, nonproprietary scholarship divorced from revenue considerations, and faculty control of the curriculum. As the academy has moved to a more market-oriented approach in both its governance and operation, the critics have charged that these new approaches leave faculty "out of the [governance] loop" (Carr, 1999) and bypassed in the decision-making process (Abel, 2000). In particular, opponents of university-owned, for-profit subsidiaries have argued that the speed and manner in which these companies have been created are antithetical to the tradition and culture of shared governance (Kezar, 2001), and worry that top-down, corporate-style management is regrettably replacing traditional models of shared governance. These subsidiaries may help reinforce and speed corporate-style governance throughout a campus. As one professor commented, for-profit subsidiaries "put the standard rules of academic governance on [their] head" (Abel, 2000, p. A21).

These challenges to traditional governance may be the tip of the proverbial iceberg regarding commercial activities and have many "fearful that the university's true educational mission is being compromised" (Simpson, 2001, p. 54). Opponents of such strategies assert the growing need to "make sure that the university does not betray its educational values and objectives" (Croissant, 2001, p. 45), or worry that market-oriented activities will eventually "change the social role of higher education institutions" for the worse (Breneman, 2002). On an even darker note, former American Council on Education and University of Illinois President Stanley Ikenberry (2001) warned that "any serious weakening in the integrity of the [university] or any corruption of the academic culture could be its undoing" (p. 15). Others concur (Nelson, 1997; Slaughter, 2001; Slaughter & Leslie, 1997; Smith, 2000; Soley, 1995; Stankiewicz, 1986).

As marriages between for-profit companies and nonprofit organizations proliferated, the distinctions between these two organizational forms blur (Minow, 2000; Ryan, 1999; Weisbrod, 1997). Such unions present substantial challenges. Oster (1995) asserts that these arrangements often precipitate serious governance issues, making it "quite difficult to maintain one structure for one part of the business and a second structure for the rest of the business" (p. 96).

Though concerns about the corporatization of higher education and its governance have lately come to a head, the challenge to universities posed by outside corporate and business influence was first recognized almost 100 years ago. Thorstein Veblen railed against the university as a "corporation of learning" and labeled college presidents "captains of erudition" (as quoted in Birnbaum, 2000, p. 17). Veblen asserted that "the intrusion of business principles into the universities goes to weaken and retard the pursuit of learning, and therefore to defeat the ends for which a university is maintained" (as quoted in Birnbaum, 2000, p. 17).

Since Veblen, the debate has picked up steam, frequently manifesting itself as a battle between the classroom and the boardroom, with "students and professors on one side, and university administrators and companies ... on the other" (Noble, 1998, p. 1). For example, critics have questioned the quality of the courses offered by both for-profit universities and the new partnerships, and labeled any educational institution with a ".com" in its Internet address a "potential rip-off" (Altschuler, 2001) or "a Wal-Mart education" (Keegan, 2000, p. 1).

On the other side of the dispute, as market forces increase, other scholars and leaders assert that the academy must adapt to new market-driven realities. They argue that technology and new ways of delivering education could increase the number of students served as well as protect at-risk programs by improving the university's financial condition (Carnevale, 1999). In a challenge to higher education leaders, Jorge Klor de Alva (2000)—then president of the University of Phoenix, holder of an endowed chair at the University of California, Berkeley, and a professor of Anthropology at Princeton University—exhorted them to "rethink the rules that govern higher education today" (p. 36) and stressed that "many of the risk-averse, traditional rules of higher education are beginning to appear not merely quaint but irrelevant or even downright absurd" (p. 34).

The subsequent closure of many of these subsidiaries has sparked further controversy. The explanations for these closures tend to focus on economics. However, some have speculated that it was more a result of mismatches in governance processes and culture. One commentator blamed a subsidiary's failure on its inability to "break from its academic roots" and operate like a business, claiming that the demise of a subsidiary was because of "cultural differences" with the parent institution (Carlson & Carnevale, 2001).

Since December 1998, several major universities—including Columbia and Duke Universities, UCLA, and the University of Nebraska—have established for-profit subsidiaries, all with the express purpose of marketing and delivering education. Along with the goal of reaping the financial rewards education could provide, universities created for-profit subsidiaries to maintain or expand enrollments, to benefit from the use of technology, to expand and bolster their "brand names," and to operate outside of their parent institution's governance structures and processes (Abel, 2000; Leonhardt, 2000; Tapscott, 1999).

This chapter considers the governance challenges posed by university commercial activities through four prominent for-profit subsidiaries—NYU's *NYUonline*, Duke's *Duke Corporate Education*, Columbia's *Fathom*, and Babson College's *Babson Interactive*. Because of space limitations and to illustrate more vividly the challenges of governing these entrepreneurial activities, the chapter looks closely at only two of these companies through short case studies. The two cases represent the biggest differences between the four companies and highlight the issues that are at play in each of these companies to varying degrees. The chapter then identifies several paradoxes encountered in the governance and operation of these organizations and concludes with an exploration of key insights for administrative and faculty leaders and trustees. In essence, the chapter provides a window into whether it is possible for the academy to "do business like a business"—a trend afoot (to the dismay of many)—and still retain essential academic values.

THE CLASH OF CULTURES

As colleges and universities have embraced market values (some more quickly than others), they have adjusted their governance structures and processes, and altered their cultures accordingly, often excluding faculty from key committees and isolating them from all but the most clear-cut academic and curricular issues

(Carlson, 2000a; Van Der Werf & Blumenstyk, 2001; Zusman, 1999). These adjustments prompted one commentator to proclaim, "Universities themselves are beginning to look and behave like for-profit companies" (Press & Washburn, 2000, p. 46).

Organizational culture is an important lens to understand the governance tensions between academic institutions and their for-profit entities. Organizational culture can be defined as "a core set of assumptions, understandings, and implicit rules that govern day-to-day behavior in the workplace" (Deal & Kennedy, 1982, p. 4) ; "those elements of a group or organization that are most stable and least malleable" (Schein, 1992, p. 5); "a set of commonly held attitudes, values, and beliefs that guide the behavior of an organization's members" (Martin, 1985, p. 148); and "the way we do things around here" (Arnold & Capella, 1985, p. 32). Regardless of specific definition, an organization's culture shapes its policies, processes, and structure, and thereby provides a foundation for governance (Masland, 1991).

Additionally, as these definitions imply, values form the foundation of organizational culture, thus ultimately, the controversy over commercialization in the academy is about values. Richard Posner (2002) argued that commercialization has caused colleges and universities to "lose their souls." Similarly, condemning the current trajectory of higher education, James Perley, chair of the American Association of University Professors, asserted that such practices will "destroy the tradition of higher education as a community of scholars" (as quoted in Wilms & Zell, 2002). Another commented, "Private money is spreading through universities like a stain—infecting independent institutions with commercial values" (Ahuja, 2001).

It is in values that the corporation and academy most differ (Schein, 1992). Higher education espouses the values of professional autonomy and academic freedom. In conjunction with these reside several basic assumptions: the unfettered pursuit of "truth"; the discovery of knowledge for its own sake, for social good, and for public benefit; and the sharing, rather than hoarding, of knowledge (Austin, 1990). Along with these lies the basic assumption, particularly among faculty, that the institution is a "community of scholars who work together to govern the institution" (Austin, 1990, p. 62). Thus, shared governance, with its assumptions of widespread consultation and decision making through consensus, is one of the basic assumptions and central tenets of the academy.

Conversely, basic assumptions in for-profit organizations include capitalism, the pursuit of profit, the discovery of knowledge for competitive advantage, and the patenting and hoarding of knowledge for commercial purposes. Additionally, the for-profit sector prizes market-oriented decision making, efficient operations, cost reduction, and accountability for results. In contrast to governance by a community of scholars, for-profit corporations are typically governed by a clear hierarchy (Oster, 1995). Colleges are ideally collegial in nature, whereas corporations are managerial (Millett, 1962).

Drucker (1989) articulated a key distinction between governance in for-profits and nonprofits, which underscores cultural incongruencies: "The businesses I work with start their planning with financial returns. The nonprofits start with the performance of their missions" (p. 89). Oster (1995) asserted that a nonprofit's mission and organizational values are "quite central to management in a way that it is often not in the corporate world" (p. 12). However, many proclaim that universities should be run more like businesses (Myers, 2001; Willis, 2001) and argue that nonprofit colleges and universities should shift their governance practices from the traditional shared governance of the academy, which some term "unworkable" (Ruch, 2001, p. 153), to the more hierarchical and market-oriented practices of the corporate world. This shift, which impacts the traditional values and mission of the nonprofit university, is at the heart of the controversy over the creation of for-profit subsidiaries in nonprofit higher education.

A TALE OF TWO SUBSIDIARIES

To document the governance tensions of commercial entities and their non-profit academic hosts, I conducted case studies of two for-profit subsidiaries established by higher education institutions to deliver distance education. The short descriptions that follow—describing the experience of *NYUonline* and *Babson Interactive*—confirm the centrality of governance and culture in these ventures and identify several paradoxes that highlight governance challenges in an increasingly commercialized academy.

NYUonline, Inc

New York University created NYUonline in 1998 as a for-profit company with several objectives: (1) the hope of financial return and access to needed capital, (2) the desire to be free from the university's governance structure, and (3) as a means of retaining and capitalizing its faculty's intellectual property. NYU considered itself a very entrepreneurial university. Accordingly, there was little objection to NYUonline's creation. The company's initial business plan was to help the university produce online courses and deliver them to individual students of all types and at all levels—both degree and nondegree, graduate and undergraduate. However, after a year, it shifted its strategy to focus exclusively on providing online, noncredit training to corporations. This change in direction occurred shortly after a change in NYUonline's management. It replaced continuing education administrators with a team of business executives who had ample media publishing and e-commerce expertise, but no experience as academic administrators. The distance learning administrators who had managed the company during its first year of operation were transferred to NYU's nonprofit continuing education department, where they produced credit-bearing distance learning courses. NYUonline's headquarters was moved to an off-campus office building.

Along with this new executive team, NYUonline was governed by a seven-member board of directors, which included three university trustees—all very accomplished business executives—and four key university administrators.

NYUonline's chief executive reported directly to one of these trustees on an operational basis, while ultimately being accountable to the board as a whole. However, he had only an indirect reporting relationship to the university. No faculty members were on the company's board of directors. The university's president was not on the board of directors in order to safely distance himself from the company in case of an adverse reaction by the university's faculty to the company's operations. Though a faculty advisory board was considered, it was never established, and because of the noncredit nature of the course materials the company produced, faculty were not involved at all in governing the company.

The university's central administration limited NYUonline's management team from directly contacting the university's faculty to participate in course production and delivery, and instead required them to access faculty after first speaking with and receiving approval from the appropriate dean. Because, prior to NYUonline's founding, the university's central administration had provided no explanation of the company's purpose, scope, and operation, each dean was wary about what participating or not participating with the company meant for them politically in the university. Many were also skeptical about the company's management and its operations. The prohibition from contacting the university's faculty directly left NYUonline's management in a constant position of trying to negotiate with the deans, and continually working to establish their own and the company's legitimacy and trustworthiness, all with little help from NYU's central administration.

After two years of operation, NYU's board of trustees decided against reinvesting in the company, effectively closing NYUonline.

Babson Interactive

Babson College, near/in Boston established Babson Interactive as an institutional strategy to perpetuate what it considers as its core mission: to not only teach, but to embody entrepreneurship in business. College officials also hoped the company would develop into a profitable business. The college's dean of graduate and executive education founded the company and became its chief executive. Faculty were consulted in the company's creation (though not part of the decision process). From its outset, Babson Interactive set out to create and deliver both credit and non–credit bearing courses for use in executive education and graduate business programs, including its own degree programs.

Babson Interactive was governed by a board that included two of the college's trustees, the college's president, a current faculty member, the company's legal counsel, the college's chief operating officer (who was a former faculty member), and Babson Interactive's chief executive (who also retained his position as dean of executive education). The company's chief executive reported directly to the college's president rather than to the chair of Babson Interactive's board. Many of Babson Interactive's top managers were alumni of the college and some were even former professors. All had a connection and familiarity with the college prior to their employment. The company was headquartered on Babson's campus.

In addition to the board of directors, the company established two faculty oversight boards that reported to Babson College's curriculum committee. These boards were charged with monitoring the design and quality of the credit-bearing courses Babson Interactive produced and with the oversight of various faculty issues, including workload.

In Babson Interactive's early existence, Babson College faculty worked to produce (and eventually deliver) online courses and other materials for the company under only handshake agreements. This work was done in addition to an individual professor's normal workload. Because a formal set of contracts had not been developed, the relationship between Babson Interactive and these professors was solely based on trust and good faith. Later, employment contracts were formalized, but with or without a contract, Babson faculty were engaged in the work of the subsidiary from the outset.

Babson Interactive continues to operate, although hurt by the recent downturn in the national economy. However, it has been folded into the institution and is no longer a for-profit university subsidiary.

CULTURAL OUTLIER OR CULTURAL EXTENSION?

As these brief case descriptions illustrate, organizational culture mattered a great deal in developing workable relationships between the entrepreneurial activity and the host parent institution of these two for-profit subsidiaries. For Babson College, the subsidiary embodied the institution, in effect became a "statement of values" (Chait, Holland, & Taylor, 1993, p. 24) and served "to exemplify and reinforce the organization's core values" (p. 9). Babson Interactive symbolically reinforced the college's identity and sense of self—"we are entrepreneurial"—and signaled to outside constituencies the institution's willingness to try new things and to practice what it preached. In fact, one could conjecture that if Babson had not created the subsidiary, its constituents might easily have questioned why the college had not entered the online education market when so many others had. Inaction by the college, at a time when postsecondary entrepreneurial activity was proliferating all around it, would have been incongruent with Babson's culture and could have potentially caused more problems than creating the subsidiary did.

Conversely, NYUonline was a cultural incongruity, insulated and separate from the parent institution in many ways. The subsidiary was quarantined, in effect, in order to safeguard the traditional culture of the university and to remove the company from the university's traditional governance protocols, even though NYU is considered by many to be highly entrepreneurial. Without a separation of the subsidiary from the parent institution, both entities ran the risk that either the traditional academic governance model would be imposed on the subsidiary or that the subsidiary's corporate approach would spill into the university. Especially with respect to access to the NYU faculty, it seemed that the academic community had to be assured that there was no risk of infection. NYUonline was in essence a contained experiment developed with a thicker membrane between the parent and the subsidiary to keep governance challenges distinct and at bay because each viewed the other as very different from itself. Senior administrators actively worked to reinforce these differences.

At Babson College, the subsidiary was a close next-of-kin to the parent culturally, so there was no danger of contagion, less need for distance, and subsequently, more similarity between the two institutions. The traditional academic culture and processes and those of the new venture looked familiar to the other. In fact, the two organizations shared the same cultural DNA and thus enjoyed a symbiotic existence.

In sum, the greater the disparity in culture between the parent and the subsidiary, the more difficult it was to create necessary linkages between the two. Although NYUonline was clearly a governance outlier, insulated from NYU because of its divergent culture, Babson Interactive followed the cultural pedigree of its parent and was merely an extension of the college into the marketplace.

ISOLATION OR INTEGRATION—THE KEY GOVERNANCE QUESTION

By expanding this conversation to include two additional subsidiaries— Fathom, whose fate was most similar to NYUonline's, and Duke Corporate Education, which most closely resembled Babson Interactive—one can better understand how different cultures and values affect the relationship between host institution and commercial activity and alleviate (or contribute) to potential governance tensions. In fact, contrary to what was considered crucial for success, the subsidiaries that had the most connections to their parents' structures and process, and, in particular, their culture and values, seemed to enjoy the most success. In essence, those that had a better "fit" seemed to fare better.

The degree of divergence from the parent culture had a profound effect on and important consequences for the subsidiaries. When viewed through the lens of organizational culture, the potential difficulties encountered in governing the for-profit company vis-à-vis the nonprofit university become clearer. These difficulties are reflected vividly in the robustness of each subsidiary. Interestingly, regardless of cultural commonalties, none of these four subsidiaries exists today in the form that each was first created. In fact, only Duke Corporate Education still endures as a distinct organization, though it is currently in the process of moving from for-profit to nonprofit status. Fathom and NYUonline both were closed, and Babson Interactive was folded back into the operations of Babson College.

Administrators overseeing Fathom and NYUonline attributed their closures to economic conditions, but their failure may, in fact, have resulted from a mismatch between the for-profit, corporate culture of the subsidiary and the traditional academic culture of the parent university (Carlson & Carnevale, 2001). In particular, one commentator argued that the for-profit subsidiary and nonprofit university "seem to be impossible combinations" because of the "fundamental difference in culture" between the two organizations (Wilson, 2003, p. 7). Thus, the demise

Figure 3.1
Cultural Fit Continuum

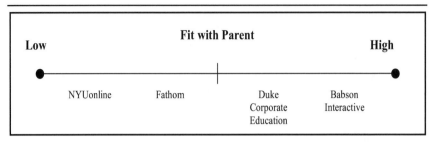

of these companies may have been caused more by problems of culture than by problems of capital and markets—a consequence of fit, not finances.

A closer look at the cultural fit between each parent and subsidiary is helpful here (see Figure 3.1). The two institutions with the least congruity, NYUonline and Fathom, closed. Furthermore, NYUonline, which most diverged from its parent's culture, had the shortest lifespan. In the case of the other two subsidiaries, Duke CE, though struggling somewhat—in October 2001, Duke Corporate Education laid off 10 of 77 employees (Mangan, 2001)—has been profitable at times and has been ranked #1 in the world in customized corporate education by both *Business Week* and *The Financial Times*. Babson Interactive did not exhibit any outward signs of organizational difficulty, although the company seemed to serve its entrepreneurial purpose for the college and ultimately changed its relationship with Babson College, abandoning its for-profit status and becoming part of the institution.

These outcomes imply a systematic association between cultural congruity and the success (economic viability) of these institutions. Though a causal relationship is difficult to establish, it seems that the viability of for-profit subsidiaries relates to the degree of compatibility between the cultures of the parent and subsidiary. At the very least, congruity contributed to longevity for the subsidiaries.

Because culture dictates and defines the limits of appropriate behavior in an organization, the extent to which a subsidiary's structures, processes, values, and even personnel align with the parent culture is crucial. Birnbaum (1988) asserted:

> Organizational cultures establish the boundaries within which various behaviors and processes take place. By helping to create shared symbols, myths, and perceptions of reality, they allow participants to make sense of an equivocal world and to establish a consensus on appropriate behavior. (p. 80)

An organization that is working well is acting according to "collectively valued purposes in a proper and adequate manner" (Meyer & Rowan, 1977, p. 346) when its structures, particularly in governance, match the values of the prevailing culture. In this sense, "organizations structurally reflect socially constructed reality" (p. 346). Chaffee and Tierney (1988) contend that for an institution to reach a state of equilibrium, its structure and values must be congruent. A mismatch can cause "structural and normative contradictions within the culture" (p. 28). Without alignment, tensions result and these "contradicting valences can create serious problems in the long run" (p. 183). This situation is what we see in both NYUonline and Fathom.

When structures and values are aligned, however, a new organizational structure, or, in this case, a subsidiary, "becomes legitimate" (Meyer & Rowan, 1977, p. 349). It becomes accepted within the culture and the power structure. With legitimacy, a subsidiary organization can solidify support and improve chances for survival. In these instances, faculty and other key stakeholders accept the subsidiary as part of themselves.

> Organizations [including their sub-units] must have the confidence of their environments, not simply be in rational exchange with them. And those that have this confidence and legitimacy receive all sorts of social resources that provide for success and stability. (Meyer & Rowan, 1978, p. 107)

Entrepreneurial activities that do not incorporate culturally acceptable elements of their institution's structure lack legitimacy and become "more vulnerable to claims that they are ... unnecessary" (Meyer & Rowan, 1977, p. 350), or even potentially dangerous to the parent organization. Thus, the success of for-profit subsidiaries may depend as much on legitimacy derived from congruency between structures and values as on financial and market considerations. Where subsidiaries are viewed as illegitimate and incongruent with the culture of their institution, potential tensions exist that will manifest in governance conflicts.

The extent to which the for-profit subsidiary and the parent institution were separated from each other reflected a judgment by administrators of the parent institution and managers of the subsidiary as to the danger of contagion or cultural contamination between the subsidiary and parent. The resulting governance structures and processes and the problems they created were a byproduct of this judgment.

EXPERIMENTATION OR CONTINUITY: LOOSE AND TIGHT COUPLING

Institutions continually test the waters of new revenue streams. In this situation, each for-profit subsidiary had an "experimental" quality. As experiments, these subsidiaries illustrate Weick's (1976; 1990) description of universities and colleges as "loosely coupled systems," where organizational elements are "responsive, but retain evidence of separateness and identity" (Weick, 1976, p. 3) and where elements affect each other "suddenly (rather than continuously), occasionally (rather than constantly), negligibly (rather than significantly), indirectly (rather than directly), and eventually (rather than immediately)" (Weick, 1982, p. 380). In loosely coupled systems, an adaptation, or experiment, deemed potentially dangerous to the organization as a whole, can be quickly and naturally quarantined, preventing system-wide infiltration (Weick, 1976). The for-profit subsidiary that is not culturally congruent with its parent can be effectively isolated from the rest of the university. Thus, without compatibility, integration becomes nearly impossible. The resulting isolation protects the parent, but dooms the subsidiary.

Weick (1976) asserts that loosely coupled systems are optimal for experimentation, or "localized adaptation" (p. 6), where changes can be made to one part of the system without effect on the whole. The university, while an "exquisite mechanism" (Weick, 1976, p. 7) for experimentation, is poorly suited to comprehensive or systemic long-term change as a result of isolated experiments. "This same loose coupling can also forestall the spread of advantageous mutations" throughout an organization (p. 7). Thus, the for-profit subsidiary can be created as an experimental response to external stimuli, but the very nature of the university may discourage the integration of the company and cross-fertilization between the company and the university.

Organizational culture can be crucial to this dialectic between experimentation and continuity. Because loose coupling inherently "carries connotations of impermanence, dissolvability, and tacitness" (Weick, 1976), some centripetal force must operate to hold the organization together. In the university, culture serves this purpose and functions as the "glue" (Tushman & O'Reilly, 1996, p. 21; Weick & Orton, 1990, p. 212) or cohesive force (Meyer & Rowan, 1977). The carriers of the culture are faculty members, who work to perpetuate a university's beliefs and values (Kuh & Whitt, 1988). In operational terms, the faculty were the key cultural connection between the loosely coupled units, in these cases between the for-profit subsidiary and parent.

Faculty serve as Weick's (1976) "technical core," a key "coupling mechanism" (p. 4). They are crucial to the success of these subsidiaries, not only because they created the products that were marketed by the companies, but because they serve as the critical cultural link as well in each company's "supply chain." Without faculty expertise, the company could not compete in the marketplace. Yet, managers at NYUonline and Fathom were isolated from the parent university's faculty. Because each subsidiary's business centered on leveraging the university's prestige and reputation for quality, and more particularly, the faculty's knowledge and expertise to produce educational material, the greater the degree of separation, the more imperiled the business model. To produce this material these companies had to engage faculty and accommodate the pace and rhythm of the university. A complete separation might assure freedom from intrusion by the parent's shared governance processes and some degree of protection for its trustees. At the same time, separation severely limits the company's capacity to take products to the marketplace, where the demand was for a product that only faculty could produce, no matter how loosely coupled to the parent organizationally.

The faculty are, of course, critical to any university's success. Yet, as culture bearers and culture conservers, faculty can impede adaptation and change. Likewise, successful business organizations often have strong cultures with deeply ingrained norms and values that are, at once, a "critical component" of the organization's success and an obstacle to innovation and change (Tushman & O'Reilly, 1996,

p. 16). A culture of stability and consistency impedes behaviors that allow risk and ambiguity. As a result, the business literature strongly counsels managers to create subsidiary organizations in order to deal with "disruptive technologies" that may threaten an organization's core product or when the operation of the subsidiary clashes with the parent organization's values or processes (Christensen, 1997; Christensen & Overdorf, 2000; Gilbert, 2001; Gilbert & Bower, 2002; Tushman, Anderson, & O'Reilly, 1997; Tushman & O'Reilly, 1999). In essence, they advise pursuing a loose coupling strategy to avoid culture's centripetal force. With separation, these organizations are then free to operate in a new business environment and context and avoid the "work processes and decision-making patterns that may be dysfunctional in the new environment" (Gilbert & Bower, 2002). The distance gives the subsidiary organization the ability to "develop within it the new processes and values required" (Christensen & Overdorf, 2000, p. 73) to take advantage of new market opportunities.

This may not be the case in academic entrepreneurial activities. Because of the academic subsidiary's dependence on faculty, however, separation cannot be achieved, and given the examples of NYUonline and Fathom, should not be encouraged. Separating the subsidiary from the faculty, and the university's culture, proved to be its downfall. The subsidiary's dependence on faculty actually suggests the need for *tight*, not loose, coupling. Hence, Babson Interactive's close connection to its parent is a model. However, tight coupling has potential dangers as well. The close relationship means that some spillover will occur and the entrepreneurial (and thus corporate) beliefs, values, and strategies necessary for the subsidiary to succeed in the marketplace may seep into the institution. Leaders will have to monitor this exchange and determine how beneficial or detrimental it is.

Loose coupling, though suited for experimentation in higher education, creates difficulties for the long-term survival of the entrepreneurial activities. This situation creates an interesting paradox: the subsidiaries were designed to be largely independent of the university, the academic culture, and faculty governance, in order to increase economic viability; however, the subsidiaries with the most separation were the least viable. In effect, the less culturally recognizable the subsidiary was to the parent, the less likely the organization would survive. This does not conform with the prevailing thought in the business world, where the opposite is true—where the goal is to create a unit culturally foreign and unrecognizable to the parent. In the university, however, an alien academic subsidiary will, in many cases, be isolated and rejected.

IT'S A TRICKY BUSINESS: PERILOUS PARADOXES

In sum, the experiences of these subsidiaries reveal three potentially debilitating paradoxes that lie at the heart of governance.

First, academic culture is very powerful and calls for academic administrators to operate and govern business activities, yet these same academic administrators may not be suited to operate the business in a way that will ensure survival in the highly competitive world of for-profit education.

Second, faculty are needed to have a close connection to these businesses in order to provide appropriate content and educational material that will meet the needs of the market and to serve as cultural bridges between the institution and the new enterprise. However, a close connection to faculty largely tends to require that the business operate on a different time orientation that is incongruent with the "get it to me yesterday" demands of the competitive marketplace.

Finally, the key paradox found in the operation and demise of the for-profit subsidiary was the idea that separation from governance and culture was essential for economic survival. In the end, just the opposite was true. The more separate, the faster the downfall. Though one of the original aims of those creating these subsidiaries was to circumvent and avoid traditional academic governance, this was never totally achieved and the degree to which it was may have been detrimental to the companies, particularly in the case of NYUonline. This casts doubt on the for-profit subsidiary's ability to separate from its parent's academic culture and governance, and raises serious questions about the wisdom in attempting to do so. In essence, because governance and culture are so intertwined, circumventing governance means circumventing culture—or at least attempting to, which can be a very difficult proposition because of the power of culture–and in turn, dooming the activity. Rather, academic leaders need to cultivate and nurture points of contact and interaction, particularly between the company and the faculty that supplies its educational product. Without faculty, the carriers of academic culture and producers of content knowledge, these subsidiaries will not survive. Thus, integration, rather than insulation, is the best policy.

LESSONS FOR LEADERS

These paradoxes yield important implications for trustees, administrators, and faculty when governing in an increasingly market-oriented and commercialized academy.

Culture Matters

The clearest implication concerns the importance and power of organizational culture. Despite literature that exhorts leaders to pay attention to culture (Chaffee & Tierney, 1988; Davis, 1984; Deal & Kennedy, 1982; Kotter & Heskett, 1992; Kuh & Whitt, 1988; Masland, 1991; Peters & Waterman, 1982; Schein, 1992, 1999; Tierney, 1991, 1999), academic administrators and managers of for-profit subsidiaries often neglect institutional culture. In fact they work to minimize its influence. Regarding entrepreneurial activities, Tierney's (1999) assertion holds true:

> Decision-makers usually move structures around, discuss personnel, and draw up a battle plan or "strategy," and, as they head out the door, they point out

that they need to massage the culture to make this happen.... Culture is the stepchild of decision-making; individuals work on it when they have time. (p. 154)

Paying more careful attention to culture in the governance and management of entrepreneurial activities may yield important dividends and avert nettlesome problems. Culture must be considered in the subsidiary's design and governance and not merely be relegated to a managerial afterthought. As important as competitive strategy may be to a particular activity's success, how the subsidiary fits with the parent organization may be more significant. A plan built around dollar signs may seem anomalous to higher education institutions and their cultures that thrive on shared values, and seem to hinder the entrepreneurial activity. However, not only the subsidiary's strategy, but it and the patent institution's cultures, must be thoughtfully considered. The values, assumptions, and beliefs of the institution and its subsidiary must be assessed and harmonized to the fullest extent possible. Following this evaluation, the subsidiary needs to be positioned and rationalized in a way that makes sense to the parent culture and positioned strategically in the marketplace. This dual strategy may not be possible in all situations, but those who cannot manage this balancing act should tread softly. The prospects for success seem far brighter where the subsidiary is an outgrowth of the parent culture and not an escape hatch.

Integration and Insulation

Because of the power of academic culture and the fundamental dependence on faculty, administrative leaders should work to create meaningful points of connection between the subsidiary and institution—to integrate rather than insulate. Insulation breeds suspicion and opposition; while integration allows the parent culture to take root and ultimately legitimate the subsidiary.

It is important that integration occur, but where in the institution it occurs is also important. In practical terms, given a choice of whether to create the subsidiary as a unit closely connected to a university's central administration and board of trustees or as a spin-off from the business school or some other entity, leaders should recognize the clear cultural benefit of a link to a business school or other academic unit whose culture and values are more compatible with a subsidiary whose goal is profitability. Case in point: Though Columbia and Duke are both prestigious research institutions, because Duke CE emerged from the Fuqua School of Business, it looked different from Fathom, and each company had a very different fate. Duke CE had a natural alignment with Fuqua's goals, values, and culture, and relied on academic administrators, not outside managers, to direct it. These two elements provided a strong foundation and grounding that Fathom lacked. Babson Interactive was not created from a graduate business school but, then, Babson College *is* a business school.

Nurturing connections that allow cultural crossover between parent and subsidiary reaps significant benefits. Rather than retard the work of the company, close connections enhance the subsidiary's legitimacy. Without that credibility, subsidiaries are severely handicapped.

People Are Culture Bearers

The business literature advocates that subsidiary companies be staffed with a "heavyweight team" (Christensen & Overdorf, 2000, p. 75)—people who bring "outside perspectives" (Gilbert, 2001, p. 292) to the new organization, free from the ingrained assumptions and values of the core business. These outside managers "allow the project to be governed by different values" than the parent organization and are given autonomy and authority "so that new processes and new ways of working together can emerge" (Christensen & Overdorf, 2000, p. 75).

This is imprudent advice for academic organizations. At NYUonline and Fathom, hiring a "heavyweight" management team accentuated the differences between the corporate and academic cultures. Unfamiliar with academic culture, these outside managers were puzzled by the university's "way of doing things." In the end, these managers were foreign tissue rejected by the host organism or, at least, like American executives abroad, unable to adapt to the operative norms of a foreign culture.

Perhaps, academic administrators may be more adept than career business executives at managing a university's for-profit subsidiaries. Experienced academic administrators "speak the language" of the academy, know the culture, and have credibility with faculty. Unlike the argument of the business literature, the "natives," not the newcomers, are better positioned to move between academe and business.

If, however, business executives are chosen to manage a subsidiary, the task of integration between the for-profit subsidiary and nonprofit university may rest with a mediator. This "active integrator" (Gilbert, 2001, p. 291) must work to "protect and legitimize" (Tushman & O'Reilly, 1999, p. 21) the subsidiary, and, more important, to bridge cultural differences between the parent and subsidiary. Columbia's executive vice provost, Michael Crow, performed this function for Fathom and Columbia. Fathom's CEO commented that he "[decoded] Columbia" for her (Blumenstyk, 2001) and helped her in "waters [she] didn't know how to navigate." In fact, Crow may have been so crucial to Fathom's relationship with Columbia that shortly after he left Columbia, Fathom was shut down.

No one played the mediator role effectively for NYUonline, a gap the CEO of NYUonline cited as a reason the company closed. Duke CE and Babson Interactive did not require a specific person to serve as an integrator because the fit was much tighter. Thus, this role was less essential, and it was filled by many people spanning the boundaries between parent and subsidiary. Both companies' CEOs were products of the parent organization's culture and values. They facilitated effective communication and interaction. There was no foreign tissue to reject because the gene pool was the same as the parent organism.

Business in the Academy

The closing of many of these for-profit subsidiaries suggests a central lesson for the management and governance of universities. The very ability to close these subsidiaries, lay off personnel, and cease operations sharply illustrates how businesslike universities can be (and ultimately how detached the subsidiaries may be from the faculty's concerns). Unlike the typical academic program, these programs were closed with little resistance or controversy (Eckel, 2003). There were no tortured deliberations by academic committees, no tenured faculty to relocate, and no student protests to endure. The decision was made and implemented.

These subsidiaries demonstrate that even in the academy, you make money, lose money, and move on. Universities are quite familiar with the first two, but have never been able to move on very easily. When stopping something, particularly academic in nature, governance is measured and process rich. However, the fate of these subsidiaries provided concrete examples that the academy can do business like a business. Alert presidents and trustees will recognize this. The irony is that the closure of NYUonline and Fathom was so easy because the companies were so disconnected from faculty. Stated otherwise, they were positioned squarely within the faculty's zone of indifference. Tighter coupling, ironically, will make closure more difficult.

REFERENCES

Abel, D. (2000, June 15). UMass weighs Internet push. *The Boston Globe*, pp. A1, A21.

Ahuja, A. (2001, May 7). When corporate cash corrupts. *The Times*, Section 2, p. 10–11.

Altschuler, G. C. (2001, August 5). The e-learning curve. *The New York Times*, p. 13.

Arnold, D. R., & Capella, L. M. (1985). Corporate culture and the marketing concept: A diagnostic instrument for utilities. *Public Utilities Fortnightly*, *118*(8), 32–38.

Austin, A. E. (1990). Faculty cultures, faculty values. In W. G. Tierney (Ed.), *Assessing academic climates and cultures* (pp. 61–74). San Francisco: Jossey-Bass.

Birnbaum, R. (1988). *How colleges work: The cybernetics of academic organization and leadership* (1st ed.). San Francisco: Jossey-Bass.

Birnbaum, R. (2000). *Management fads in higher education: Where they come from, what they do, why they fail*. San Francisco: Jossey-Bass.

Bleak, J. L. (2005). *When for-profit meets nonprofit: Educating through the market*. New York: Routledge Falmer.

Blum, A. (2002, June 16). Online ed taking off. *The Boston Globe*, p. H1.

Blumenstyk, G. (2001, February 9). Knowledge is 'a form of venture capital' for a top Columbia administrator. *The Chronicle of Higher Education*, p. A29.

Breneman, D. W. (2002, June 14). For colleges, this is not just another recession. *The Chronicle of Higher Education*, p. B7.

Carlson, S. (2000a, April 14). A 1,000-acre incubator for research and business. *The Chronicle of Higher Education*, pp. A49–A50, A52.

Carlson, S. (2000b, May 5). Going for profit and scholarship on the web. *The Chronicle of Higher Education*, p. A45.

Carlson, S., & Carnevale, D. (2001, December 14). Debating the demise of NYUonline. *The Chronicle of Higher Education*, p. A31.

Carnevale, D. (1999, October 22). Distance education can bolster the bottom line, a professor argues. *The Chronicle of Higher Education*, p. A60.

Carr, S. (1999, December 17). For-profit venture to market distance-education courses stirs concern at Temple. *The Chronicle of Higher Education*, p. A46.

Chaffee, E. E., & Tierney, W. G. (1988). *Collegiate culture and leadership strategies*. New York: Macmillan.

Chait, R. P., Holland, T. P., & Taylor, B. E. (1993). *The effective board of trustees*. Phoenix, AZ: American Council on Education and Oryx Press.

Christensen, C. M. (1997). *The innovator's dilemma: When new technologies cause great firms to fail*. Boston: Harvard Business School Press.

Christensen, C. M., & Overdorf, M. (2000, March-April). Meeting the challenge of disruptive change. *Harvard Business Review, 67*–76.

Croissant, J. L. (2001, September-October). Can this campus be bought? Commercial influence in unfamiliar places. *Academe, 87,* 44–48.

Davis, S. M. (1984). *Managing corporate culture*. Cambridge, MA: Ballinger.

Deal, T. E., & Kennedy, A. A. (1982). *Corporate cultures: The rites and rituals of corporate life*. Reading, MA: Addison-Wesley.

Drucker, P. (1989, July/August). What can business learn from nonprofits? *Harvard Business Review,* 88–93.

Eckel, P. D. (2003). *Changing course: Making the hard decisions to eliminate academic programs*. Westport, CT: Praeger.

Farrell, E. F. (2002, July 19). U. of Oregon offers discount on late-afternoon classes. *The Chronicle of Higher Education*, p. A33.

Frye, B. (2001, October). Racing to market. *University Business, 4,* 24.

Gilbert, C. G. (2001). *A dilemma in response: Examining the newspaper industry's response to the Internet*. Unpublished doctoral dissertation, Harvard University Graduate School of Business Administration, Boston.

Gilbert, C. G., & Bower, J. L. (2002, May). Disruptive change: When trying harder is part of the problem. *Harvard Business Review,* 94–101.

Goldstein, M. (2000, September/October). To be [for-profit] or not to be: What is the question? *Change, 33,* 25–31.

Ikenberry, S. O. (2001, Spring). The practical and the ideal: Striking a balance. *The Presidency, 4,* 15–19.

June, A. W. (2002, August 16). Checking in on campus. *The Chronicle of Higher Education*, p. A29.

Keegan, P. (2000, December). The web is transforming the university. *Business 2.0.* Retrieved from http://money.cnn.com/magazines/business2/.

Kezar, A. (2001). Seeking a sense of balance: Academic governance in the 21st century. *Association of American Colleges and Universities Peer Review, 3,* 4–8.

Klor de Alva, J. (2000, March/April). Remaking the academy. *Educause Review, 35,* 32–40.

Kotter, J. P., & Heskett, J. L. (1992). *Corporate culture and performance*. New York: Free Press.

Kuh, G. D., & Whitt, E. J. (1988). *The invisible tapestry: Culture in American colleges and universities* (ASHE-ERIC Higher Education Report No. 1). Washington, DC: ERIC Clearinghouse on Higher Education.

Kwartler, D. (2000, June). Babson & Duke form commercial enterprises. *The MBA Newsletter*, pp. 1, 4, 6.

Leonhardt, D. (2000, September 20). All the world's a campus. *The New York Times*, pp. C1, C8.

Mangan, K. S. (2001, November 14). Duke's for-profit executive-education program cuts employees to avoid a deficit. *The Chronicle of Higher Education*. Retrieved from http://chronicle.com/daily/2001/11/2001111405n.htm.

Martin, H. J. (1985). Managing specialized corporate cultures. In R. H. Kilman, M. J. Saxton, & R. Serpa (Eds.), *Gaining control of the corporate culture* (pp. 148–162). San Francisco: Jossey-Bass.

Masland, A. (1991). Organizational culture in the study of higher education. In M. Peterson, E. E. Chaffee, and T. H. White (Ed.), *Organization and governance in higher education* (4th ed.). Needham Heights, MA: Ginn Press.

Meyer, J. W., & Rowan, B. (1977). Institutionalized organizations: Formal structure as myth and ceremony. *American Journal of Sociology, 83*(2), 340–363.

Meyer, J. W., & Rowan, B. (1978). The structure of educational organizations. In M. W. Meyer (Ed.), *Environments and organizations: Theoretical and empirical perspectives* (pp. 79–109). San Francisco: Jossey-Bass.

Millett, J. D. (1962). *The academic community.* New York: McGraw-Hill.

Minow, M. (2000, March 23). *Partners not rivals?: Redrawing the lines between public and private, non-profit and profit, secular and religious.* Paper presented at the Boston University School of Law.

Myers, M. T. (2001, March 26). A student is not an input. *The New York Times*, p. A23.

Nelson, C. (1997). *Manifesto of a tenured radical.* New York: New York University Press.

Noble, D. F. (1998). *Digital diploma mills: The automation of higher education.* Retrieved July 6, 2000, from http://www.firstmonday.dk/issues/issue3_1/noble/index.html.

Oster, S. (1995). *Strategic management for nonprofit organizations.* New York: Oxford University Press.

Peters, T. J., & Waterman, R. H. (1982). *In search of excellence: Lessons from America's best-run companies.* New York: Warner Books.

Posner, R. A. (2002, June). *The university as business.* Retrieved June 10, 2002, from http://www.theatlantic.com/issues/2002/06/posner.htm.

Press, E., & Washburn, J. (2000, March). The kept university. *The Atlantic Monthly*, 39–53.

Rhoden, W. C. (2002, July 25). Oregon likes the visibility of Broadway. *The New York Times*, p. D1.

Ruch, R. (2001). *Higher ed, inc.* Baltimore: Johns Hopkins University Press.

Ryan, W. (1999, January/February). The new landscape for nonprofits. *Harvard Business Review*, 127–136.

Schein, E. H. (1992). *Organizational culture and leadership* (2nd ed.). San Francisco: Jossey-Bass.

Schein, E. H. (1999). *The corporate culture survival guide.* San Francisco: Jossey-Bass.

Simpson, E. G. (2001). University dot.com: Are we selling out? *Continuing Higher Education Review, 65*, 49–59.

Slaughter, S. (2001, September-October). Professional values and the allure of the market. *Academe, 87*, 22–26.

Slaughter, S., & Leslie, L. L. (1997). *Academic capitalism: Politics, policies, and the entrepreneurial university.* Baltimore: Johns Hopkins University Press.

Smith, C. W. (2000). *Market values in American higher education: The pitfalls and promises.* Lanham, MD: Rowman & Littlefield.

Soley, L. C. (1995). *The corporate takeover of academia.* Boston: South End Press.

Stankiewicz, R. (1986). *Academics and entrepreneurs: Developing university-industry relations*. New York: St. Martin's Press.

Suggs, W. (2000, January 14). Novel corporate deal will finance new basketball arena for U. of Maryland. *The Chronicle of Higher Education*, p. A54.

Tapscott, D. (1999, September). The new u. *The American School Board Journal, 186,* 18–20.

Tierney, W. G. (1991). Organizational culture in higher education: Defining the essentials. In M. Peterson, E. E. Chaffee, and T. H. White (Ed.), *Organization and governance in higher education* (4th ed., pp. 126–139). Needham Heights, MA: Ginn Press.

Tierney, W. G. (1999). *Building the responsive campus*. Thousand Oaks, CA: Sage Publications.

Tushman, M. L., Anderson, P., & O'Reilly, C. A. (1997). Technology cycles, innovation streams, and ambidextrous organizations: Organization renewal through innovation streams and strategic change. In M. L. Tushman & P. Anderson (Eds.), *Managing strategic innovation and change*. New York: Oxford University Press.

Tushman, M. L., & O'Reilly, C. A. (1996). Ambidextrous organizations: Managing evolutionary and revolutionary change. *California Management Review, 38*(4), 8–30.

Tushman, M. L., & O'Reilly, C. A. (1999). Building ambidextrous organizations: Forming your own "skunk works." *Health Forum Journal, 42*(2), 20–23.

Van Der Werf, M. (1999, October 15). As Coke and Pepsi do battle on campuses, colleges find a fountain of new revenue. *The Chronicle of Higher Education*, p. A41.

Van Der Werf, M., & Blumenstyk, G. (2001, March 2). A fertile place to breed businesses. *The Chronicle of Higher Education*, pp. A28–A30.

Weick, K. E. (1976). Educational organizations as loosely coupled systems. *Administrative Science Quarterly, 21,* 1–19.

Weick, K. E. (1982). Management of organizational change among loosely coupled elements. In P. S. Goodman & Associates (Eds.), *Change in organizations* (pp. 375–408). San Francisco: Jossey-Bass.

Weick, K. E., & Orton, J. D. (1990). Loosely coupled systems: A reconceptualization. *Academy of Management Review, 15*(2), 203–223.

Weisbrod, B. A. (1997). The future of the nonprofit sector: Its entwining with private enterprise and government. *Journal of Policy Analysis and Management, 16,* 541–555.

Willis, E. (2001, May 28). Why professors turn to organized labor. *The New York Times*, p. A15.

Wilms, W. W., & Zell, D. M. (2002). *Awakening the academy: A time for new leadership*. Bolton, MA: Anker.

Wilson, J. M. (2003, March). Is there a future for online ed? *University Business, 6,* p. 7.

Wojnarowski, A. (2002, August 9). *Best of times, worst of Oregon's Times Square billboard*. Retrieved August 9, 2002, from http://espn.go.com.

Zusman, A. (1999). Issues facing higher education. In P. Altbach, R. Berdahl, & P. Gumport (Eds.), *American higher education in the twenty-first century* (pp. 107–148). Baltimore: Johns Hopkins University Press.

CHAPTER 4

The Shared Decision Making in Shared Programs: The Challenges of Interinstitutional Academic Programs

Peter D. Eckel
American Council on Education

The challenge is familiar for most institutional leaders: create efficiencies and generate additional revenue so that institutions can do new things without significantly increasing costs. One strategy academic leaders frequently suggest (sometimes a bit too cavalierly) is to cooperate with other institutions to develop new academic degree programs. Cooperation, not competition, among institutions was a theme that strongly surfaced in a series of presidential roundtables sponsored by the American Council on Education and the Futures Project on competition, financing, and privatization (American Council on Education, 2005; Eckel, Couturier, & Luu, 2005). Examples of joint academic programs include Great Plains Interactive Distance Education Alliance (Great Plains IDEA), a group of 10 Midwestern research universities that joined together to offer online graduate degrees in fields related to human ecology/human sciences, and OneMBA, an international network of five business schools offering a consolidated international MBA program.

However, although hope and potential exist for interinstitutional programs, in actuality they are complicated to create and manage. In addition to decisions associated with any new degree program—such as who will teach what, and to whom—these academic joint ventures also require decisions that span institutional boundaries, add more people into the decision process, and require the consensus and ongoing involvement of faculty and administrators from all partners. This chapter explores some of the governance and decision-making challenges that arise when multiple institutions offer joint programs.

CURRICULAR JOINT VENTURES

Internal and external expectations exist for colleges and universities to offer new academic programs. Faculty are never short on ideas to develop new innovative programs and administrators seek new sources of tuition dollars. Policy makers and community and business leaders see new programs as a way to keep pace with local and regional needs. The competitive marketplace also encourages institutions to offer new programs. However, most colleges and universities continue to face ongoing fiscal constraints that limit their ability to expand offerings. The storyline is familiar: traditional sources of support such as public dollars and endowment returns are not keeping pace with institutional expenditures. The result is that institutions are trying to do more when they have insufficient funds to do so. Collaboration then becomes an appealing way to move forward (Dotolo & Strandness, 1999; Whealler Johnson & Noftsinger, 2004).

Institutions can collaborate in many ways, including in academic programs. Curricular joint ventures (CJVs) are alliances between two or more colleges or universities that result in new certificate or degree programs (Eckel, Affolter-Caine, & Green, 2003). They draw upon the resources of multiple institutions to deliver new programs to students, fill a market niche, and as a result generate (or at least do not lose) revenue. Examples of CJVs include:

- *eArmyU*—a virtual consortium of 29 two- and four-year institutions to serve the educational demands of army personnel through an extensive array of online certificate and degree programs, ranging from associate to doctoral degrees.

- *Great Plains Interactive Distance Education Alliance*—a network of 10 Midwestern research universities offering online graduate degrees in fields related to human ecology/human sciences.

- *OneMBA*—an international network of five business schools offering individual MBA degrees and a joint diploma.

- *Singapore–MIT Alliance*—a global partnership of Massachusetts Institute of Technology (MIT), the National University of Singapore (NUS), and Singapore's Nanyang Technological University (NTU) offering joint graduate degrees in advanced materials for micro- and nano-systems, high-performance computation for engineered systems, innovation in manufacturing systems and technology, molecular engineering of biological and chemical systems, and computer science.

- *Michigan Community College Virtual Learning Collaborative*—a network of all of Michigan's 28 community colleges, which collectively offers accredited courses, certificates, and degree programs online.

- *Universitas 21 Global*—an international network of 17 research universities spanning North America, Europe, Asia, and Australia and New Zealand, and in partnership with Thomson Learning, combined to form a for-profit corporation offering online professional and graduate courses, as well as MBA and MIS degrees, aimed primarily at the Asian market.

- *Virginia Tech–Wake Forest University School of Biomedical Engineering and Sciences*—a collaboration between a public and a private university in different states offering joint MS and PhD degrees in biomedical engineering, and an MD/PhD.

- *Worldwide Universities Network*—an alliance of 16 research universities from North America, Europe, and Asia that engages in research collaboration and student and faculty exchange and also offers joint academic programs in 10 areas: biomedical informatics, advanced materials and nanotechnology, green chemistry, wireless communications, nursing, geographical information systems (GIS), globalization and the geography of the new economy, earth systems, public policy and management, and Medieval studies.

The appeals of collaborative ventures are many. A summary of the joint venture literature suggests that collaborative efforts provide access to new resources and new knowledge and may open new markets for collaborative programs and services. They allow partners to extend capabilities, develop products more quickly, generate greater economies of scale, and reduce expenses (Bailey & McNally Koney, 2000; Borys & Jemison, 1989; Gulati & Singh, 1998; Hagadoorn, 1993; Whetten, 1981). Together organizations may do a better job monitoring the changing environment to understand emerging opportunities or risks (Gulati & Singh, 1998; Hagadoorn, 1993). Finally, they can offer legitimacy to individual partners when teaming with reputable and prestigious organizations (Barringer & Harrison, 2000; Oliver, 1990).

However, successful management of collaborative efforts is challenging, and they often fail. Park and Russo (1996) cite a series of studies of corporate alliances that put the failure rate of new joint ventures at between 50 and 70 percent. Although numerous challenges exist in any cooperative agreement (such as selecting the right partners, securing resources and agreeing upon alliance goals), of primary concern is how different organizations must reconcile potentially different cultures, operating procedures, and decision processes (Borys & Jemison, 1989; Rondinelli & London, 2001). Simply put: regardless of the quality of the product and the intentions of and financial support by the partners, if they cannot figure out how to work together, joint efforts are doomed. Joint academic programs may be even more challenging than other types of college and university alliances because they require faculty and administrators from multiple institutions to cooperate, they tend to be new and unfamiliar strategies, and they involve curricular decisions that often are contentious.

The focus of this chapter specifically is to explore the decision-making challenges created by and solutions for curricular joint ventures:

- What decisions do institutional partners make jointly about such academic programs? How?
- How is each partner's shared governance process involved in CJVs?
- Do CJVs complicate institutional shared governance? Does shared governance complicate CJVs?

THE SHARED GOVERNANCE OF SHARED PROGRAMS

Academic decision making on any single campus is complicated, potentially contentious, and fluid as the rules of the game are continually tested and modified. Campus governance relating to CJVs becomes even more complex because such alliances are uncharted territory for most academic leaders; partners may be unfamiliar with one another's processes and cultures and have different understandings of the environment; and, in the case of international or cross-sector alliances, partners come from different environments (Borys & Jemison, 1989). Each partner may have different expectations and norms that have to be worked through collectively. Governance of CJVs must coordinate teaching and assessment activities among partners, determining not only who is initially responsible for creating various elements associated with each, but also who is to maintain those responsibilities over time. Additionally, governance is saddled with the constant negotiation of how far each partner can reach into the curriculum and other activities jointly created and maintained, as well as those activities that are the domain of individual partners yet somewhat related to alliance activities. In fact, this point has been an issue in Universitas 21 where different unions have raised questions over the parameters of decision making. Faculty and administrators must not only work together to design and implement CJVs, but they must set up appropriate and agreeable bodies to monitor and sustain activities associated with the academic issues outlined above.

CJVs raise three particular governance issues that require attention. First, who is responsible for decision making? The long-recognized "North Star" of governance, 1966 Statement on Government, which was formed jointly by three associations representing faculty, administrators, and trustees, outlines responsibilities and activities primarily for faculty, administrators, and trustees, as well as joint responsibilities (American Association of University Professors, 2001). The Statement notes that faculty should have primary responsibility for the curriculum, and the president is largely responsible for the creation of new resources. However, the Statement's broad sweep of university issues makes it possible for various stakeholders to set their claims on the same piece of the governance pie and argue convincingly that the particular issue falls within their domain. In CJVs both administrators and faculty seem to be able to assert first rights; faculty because of their primacy in developing and overseeing the curriculum; and administrators because of their responsibility to secure revenue and design and implement new institutional arrangements. To complicate matters, the Statement does not suggest roles for external groups or provide insight on how to balance curricular matters across multiple institutions, which may be the case here. The Statement's only discussion of external relations focuses on faculty representing the institution publicly, not on creating and managing interinstitutional curricular activities. If governance on a single campus can be complicated (and possibly contentious), what will it be like when the issues and activities are shared across many partners?

The second set of shared governance decisions concerns the program, such as the courses, teaching responsibilities, instructional infrastructure and investment in it, quality assurance mechanisms, provision of necessary academic support and teaching and library resources, and awarding of degrees.

Finally, in addition to the governance issues specific to academic settings, all joint ventures are subject to concerns that apply across settings:

1. the processes through which problems are defined and solutions explored collectively (Rondinelli & London, 2001) and the means by which activities are coordinated and stability maintained (Borys & Jemison, 1989; Gulati & Singh, 1998);

2. the amount of resources invested by each partner and the obligations and distribution of returns among partners (Spekman, Forbes, Isabella & MacAvoy, 1998; Ring & Van de Ven, 1994); and

3. the extent to which each partner's governance structure has legitimacy over the shared work of the collective (Borys & Jemison, 1989), with particular attention to where individual institutional responsibility ends and collective work begins, and how much influence partners have upon other partners' institution-specific issues that may directly or indirectly relate to the alliance.

TWO CASE STUDIES IN SHARED DECISION MAKING: ONEMBA AND GREAT PLAINS IDEA

Two examples of successful curricular joint ventures are helpful in understanding the range of academic decision-making issues and how institutional leaders can develop strategies to effectively create and manage interinstitutional academic programs. OneMBA is a partnership of five business schools on four continents offering a single integrated MBA degree, and the Great Plains Interactive Distance Education Alliance (GP IDEA) is an alliance of 10 Midwestern and Western land-grant institutions offering four interinstitutional programs in fields of human sciences/human ecology. The elements presented in this chapter come from in-depth case analyses of these two alliances.

Great Plains Interactive Distance Education Alliance (Great Plains IDEA) is a network of 10 U.S. public, land-grant universities offering new online graduate degrees in the human sciences/human ecology fields. The partners include the Colleges of Human Sciences (sometimes called Colleges of Human Ecology) at Colorado State University, Iowa State University, Kansas State University, Michigan State University, Montana State University, University of Nebraska, North Dakota State University, Oklahoma State University, South Dakota State University, and Texas Tech University. The Great Plains IDEA was established in the mid-1990s to foster interinstitutional programs and cooperation. In 2001, a subset of the Great Plains IDEA institutions—Kansas State University, Montana State University, Iowa State University, South Dakota State University, North Dakota State University, Oklahoma State University, and the University of Nebraska—started an online master's degree in family financial planning. In 2003 the alliance began offering graduate degrees and certificates in gerontology, youth development, and merchandising through various configurations of partners. Students enroll in an alliance program through one of the partner institutions and must meet that institution's admission's criteria. All students, regardless of home institution, pay a common price for courses. The partners have created an income-sharing formula that distributes revenue to institutions teaching specific courses, to the student's home institution for program contributions and student services, and to the Great Plains IDEA for program coordination and joint activities such as marketing and maintaining its Web site. Students in Great Plains IDEA programs graduate with a degree from their home institution.

OneMBA is an international 21-month Executive MBA (EMBA) program that enrolled its first class in fall 2002. Partners include the Kenan-Flagler Business School of the University of North Carolina, Chapel Hill (UNC); the Rotterdam School of Management (RSM) of Erasmus University Rotterdam; the Chinese University of Hong Kong (CUHK); the Monterrey Tech Graduate School of Business Administration and Leadership (EGADE) in Mexico; and Brazil's Escola de Administração de Empresas de São Paulo—the largest of the schools that make up the Fundação Getulio Vargas (FGV). Students enroll in one of the partner institutions and pay that institution's tuition and fees. (Students tend to be working professionals who are sponsored by their employer.) The curriculum includes three components: (1) a home-institution–taught series of courses (called regional courses) that address local topics and issues, (2) a "global residency" set of week-long coordinated visits for students from all five institutions to different global regions that focus on a topic important to each specific region, and (3) a set of five globally coordinated courses taught concurrently at the partner institutions using parallel syllabi and common cases and readings. These globally coordinated courses include a team project in which small groups of students from each of the five institutions work together via technology. Upon completing their coursework, students receive MBA degrees from their home institutions. Each also receives a OneMBA diploma issued jointly by the five participating institutions.

WHAT DECISIONS DO INSTITUTIONAL PARTNERS MAKE JOINTLY ABOUT SUCH ACADEMIC PROGRAMS?

The strategic alliance literature notes that any interinstitutional activity has three key decisions to address: how it will (1) manage its coordinated operations, (2) determine partner investment in the alliance and divide returns, and (3) demarcate boundaries between alliance and partner responsibility.

Managing Operations

CJVs have both strategic and ongoing activities that require attention that can effectively be managed through a multitier approach. First, interinstitutional programs require an oversight or strategy group. Both OneMBA and Great Plains IDEA created executive committees with representation from each partner institution to oversee alliance activities and make strategic decisions. These activities included such things as determining the focus of the alliance; alliance membership; the number and types of programs and their delivery mechanisms; how to handle costs, expenses and revenue; curricular design, review, and modifications; program approval and termination; recruitment and compensation of faculty; product placement; and other issues related to the strategic direction of the alliance's shared programs. The executive committee members mostly were college administrators, although faculty were sometimes involved. The executive committees (called the Board of Directors at Great Plains IDEA and the "champions" at OneMBA) met regularly during the design of the CJV and continue to meet after the interinstitutional programs were launched.

Second, alliances require working subgroups involving a range of university administrators and faculty because developing and delivering interinstitutional programs are complex undertakings. As Debby Haynes, a faculty member from Montana State, said,

> One of the key lessons is that you [as a single administrator] cannot do this in a vacuum. You have got to get everybody on board and you have to get their investment in the process and their enthusiasm and willingness to put in the extra mile. If everybody isn't working for you [such as the registrar, the graduate deans], they could kill it in a heartbeat.

About OneMBA, Alejandro Ruelas-Gossi, the project director from Monterrey Tech, said,

> If the champion has to do everything, it is impossible. You have to empower people in universities and try to make them fall in love with the concept.

The ways an alliance develops subgroups will differ, depending on the type of help needed and consent required by the various partners. For example, in addition to a deans' oversight group, OneMBA developed subgroups to address particular shared functions, such as marketing, information technology, and logistics. Great Plains IDEA organized its subgroups by administrative position so that the registrars met and worked together, as did the graduate deans, and the chief financial officers, for example. For the most part, the participants of these subgroups were different from members of the executive committees. However, some overlap existed in OneMBA as one of its executive committee members, an expert in international marketing, participated in the marketing subgroup.

An additional set of key working groups comprised faculty to develop joint curricula and courses. In OneMBA, the executive committee (who, for the most part, held faculty rank) developed the structural framework for the curriculum with the three components—the global residencies, the globally coordinated courses, and the regional courses—and identified topics for each component. It then charged five faculty teams to develop and deliver each globally coordinated course. Great

Plains IDEA pursued a different strategy and turned over all curricular development to faculty teams for each of its three programs. This difference in approach might be explained by the fact that OneMBA focused on delivering a single MBA program, an area in which all of the "champions" had extensive experience, and Great Plains IDEA wanted to create a infrastructure that would allow for multiple interinstitutional degree programs across a range of human science fields. That said, both CJVs brought faculty together face-to-face to develop either specific programs (as with OneMBA with the globally coordinated courses) or program curricula (as with Great Plains IDEA with its three degree programs). In OneMBA, the executive committee gave the faculty teams parameters within which to work, such as 60–70 percent course overlap, the IT infrastructure, and the virtual global teams. Great Plains IDEA was not as prescriptive, only alerting faculty teams to the minimum number of credits allowable for a master's degree offered across multiple institutions and informing them of the types and levels of technology available.

Regardless of working group structure, it is very important that faculty have the ability to shape and influence the direction of the shared academic programs. Without faculty voice, these curricular alliances would have quickly stalled. Said University of Nebraska faculty member Sheran Cramer,

> This was not an idea that the administrators said to us as faculty, "OK, faculty we want you to sit together and design this program." The idea initiated with the faculty…. Throughout the process it has been under-girded by strong administrator support. If it had been a top-down administrator design or even suggestion, it might not have had the momentum from the faculty that it did.

These programs cannot be seen as administrative efforts to simply pursue additional revenue. Said one campus administrator from Kansas State University,

> The program content originated with the faculty and not with the administration. Trying to sell eight different faculties on something that [comes from] top-down type management would never work. If it is hard enough to do that with one [faculty curriculum committee] you sure can't do it with eight.

Third, working groups are important to managing operations, but CJVs also benefit from written and agreed-upon guiding principles that outline parameters and set responsibilities. The Great Plains IDEA principles were suggested by the working group of graduate deans and later adopted by the whole. The OneMBA principles were created by the executive committee. Both sets of principles address issues such as the contributions each institution would make to the academic programs and to alliance management, how curricular content will be developed and agreed upon, and responsibilities for student recruitment and coordination among partners. Other topics specific to each alliance, particularly the international nature of OneMBA and the multiple degrees offered by Great Plains IDEA, were additionally addressed. The guiding principles are listed in Table 4.1.

Great Plains IDEA developed a handbook in addition to its principles that outlined bylaws and key policies. The bylaws state the purpose of the alliance; define

Table 4.1
Executive Board Guiding Principles

Great Plains IDEA	OneMBA
Principle 1: The participating graduate schools mutually respect the academic standards and quality of the academic departments involved in this joint program, therefore:	1. Our goal is to build one of the premier branded Global Executive MBA Programs in the world.
1. Courses approved for delivery by this program will be considered interinstitutional courses and will be exempt from transfer credit policies.	2. The program must be marketable in each region. The design and pricing must generate enough students in each school to sustain an independent section.
2. Faculty members who provide instruction in this program must carry graduate faculty status at their home institution; however, further documentation or approval will not be required by other members of the Alliance.	3. The pricing and number of students in regions do not need to be the same. The design should be similar enough to co-brand the program.
3. Students admitted as degree-seeking students in Great Plains IDEA programs will be automatically accepted by all other members of the Alliance for enrollment in courses that are part of the curricula of Great Plains IDEA programs. Admissions to a Great Plains IDEA program will be based upon the criteria established by each participating institution and program prerequisites established for the Alliance program to which admission is sought. Institutions are encouraged not to require the GRE.	4. To maximize global networking and students learning from each other, the program will facilitate global interaction among students and create the feel of one global class.
	5. Core course material will be done in the home country, but coordinated across schools.
	6. The travel to regions is designed to give students an understanding of different business models, cultures, and regulatory environments. The trips will focus on regional comparisons, regional specialization, and student interaction. Trips will have a strong link to academic component while focusing on experiential learning.
4. The number of students that may be admitted to the program by each participating institution will be determined by agreement of the participating institutions.	7. The home university will manage their program, revenue and costs, unless it involves key common costs or common issues for the partnership. The schools will contribute to a common fund in an equitable manner to cover the common cost and governance of the program.
5. The content of the curriculum will be determined by agreement of the participating institutions.	

Table 4.1
Executive Board Guiding Principles (*Continued*)

Great Plains IDEA	OneMBA
Principle 2: The participating graduate schools recognize that the implementation of Great Plains IDEA programs at each institution may be best accomplished using procedures and practices that are inherent to those respective institutions, therefore:	8. We will strongly encourage faculty coordination of our common core courses and reward faculty innovation in developing global team projects and cases. However, we will not force coordination where it is not productive.

Principle 2: The participating graduate schools recognize that the implementation of Great Plains IDEA programs at each institution may be best accomplished using procedures and practices that are inherent to those respective institutions, therefore:

1. The Great Plains IDEA programs may be stand-alone majors, emphases, options, or some other designation, as appropriate to the respective universities.
2. A student in Great Plains IDEA programs who is degree seeking will enroll in all cross-listed Alliance courses at the home institution. Elective courses within the program may or may not be cross listed.
3. The admissions procedures for students seeking degrees will be determined by their home institution, within the standards and limitations on numbers agreed to by the participating institutions.
4. Each university is responsible for obtaining initial approval and approval of any subsequent changes in the program, through the [governance] processes that are in place and required by their respective institutions.
5. Each institution will provide a transcript for courses taught by faculty at partner institutions, as it deems appropriate, consistent with the guidelines indicated in Principle 1.

Principle 3: The participating graduate schools commit to minimize the unique challenges and barriers for students that might otherwise occur in an interinstitutional distance education program to the extent possible, therefore:

8. We will strongly encourage faculty coordination of our common core courses and reward faculty innovation in developing global team projects and cases. However, we will not force coordination where it is not productive.
9. We will work together to apply the appropriate use of distance learning, but not at the expense of a rigorous program.
10. English will be the common language of the program and all participants (faculty and students) must be able to communicate effectively in English. Home university courses may use materials in the home language when not available in English.
11. The partners have no current conflicts with our Executive MBA Program and will discuss with all the partners any future potential conflicts with our program as they arise.
12. Because this will be the premier executive MBA program for each of our schools, the good of the partnership will come before the good of the individual schools.
13. The broader goal of the partnership is to find additional ways to share knowledge and resources, to gain scale economics in tackling new educational challenges and to further leverage the strengths of this partnership.
14. The program will be designed to contain the potential for adding more partners. Partners commit to having another partner in a distinct part of their region if that is the judgment of the other partners.

Table 4.1
Executive Board Guiding Principles (*Continued*)

Great Plains IDEA	OneMBA
1. A student will apply and be admitted to one Alliance institution that will become that student's home institution. All student services will be provided by that student's home institution. Students will enroll in all Alliance courses through their home institution.	15. The partners agree to regular meetings of at least once a year. The program design will include an emphasis on flexibility to allow continuous improvement.
2. Each institution will facilitate the exchange of information relative to courses completed and grades earned consistent with Federal regulations for the release of information.	
3. A common database of student and course information will be established by the Great Plains IDEA to facilitate the transfer of student and course information between home institution and the teaching institution.	

and outline the responsibilities of the lead institution; and discuss membership qualifications, affiliations, and termination (voluntary and involuntary); the roles of the board of directors; officers; project approval procedures; fiscal management; and dissolution. The handbook addresses alliance policies regarding membership (including termination), governance and the responsibilities of alliance officers, alliance and program operations, program faculty, and curricular and student issues. Neither group sought approval for its principles or bylaws from any on-campus body other than university general council for legal advice.

In addition to the leadership and coordination provided by the Great Plain IDEA's executive board, it formally designated one of its partner institutions as the "Lead Institution" through an application and voting process. The Lead Institution is responsible for managing the alliance's finances, including collecting and expending funds and maintaining correct and complete books and records of accounts. It also is responsible for coordinating alliance activities. OneMBA did not formally designate a partner institution to this role, although UNC, as the initiating school, initially acted as lead institution.

Financing the CJV

In any type of relationship, tensions can easily surface over money. The same is true in joint academic programs. CJVs can either adopt a common tuition pricing structure (Great Plains IDEA) whereby students, regardless of the partner institution through which they enroll, pay one price, or they can decentralize pricing, allowing each institution to set its own tuition and fees. In either case, partners must develop a cost-sharing strategy to support alliance activities.

Great Plains IDEA pursued a common pricing strategy ($350 per credit for 2003–2004). The mechanics are such that students write one check to their home institution regardless of which institution is teaching the courses. The home institution then disperses the income according to a formula that roughly follows an indirect cost model for sponsored research: 12.5 percent admitting/home university (where the student enrolls to cover student-service costs such as advising, admission, graduation clearance, and so forth); 12.5 percent to the alliance to support joint activities; and 75 percent to the teaching university.

OneMBA took a different approach. Instead of common pricing, it chose to let each partner set its own price. Each institution in OneMBA kept all of its revenue and the partners were responsible for their individual costs and agreed upon joint expenditures. This approach reflected one of their guiding principles about developing a program that is appealing in different parts of the world. For instance, a price that works in North America or Europe might put OneMBA out of reach in Latin America.

To determine their individual prices, each OneMBA partner followed its own past practices. Said Penny Oslund, Executive Director of EMBA Programs at UNC, "We tried to establish a price—because our programs have to be run as receipt-supported—that covered our costs and kept the price as reasonable as possible." Mexico's Monterrey Tech Graduate School of Business Administration and Leadership (EGADE) followed a more informal process. Said EGADE's Ruelas-Gossi,

> I just added $4,000 to the most expensive [program] in Mexico.... People are not that sensitive to the prices. Because a company agrees to support someone, [the exact price] doesn't make a difference for a big company.

The other key financial decision is how to cover start-up costs that can be supported by partner contributions, through external support, or a combination of both. OneMBA partners agreed make an initial contribution (USD$20,000). However, alliance leaders realized, after their first year of operating, that not all costs are shared equally among the partners because they operate in different global markets, have different expenditures and varying needs. They altered their financial infrastructure so that some expenses are divided on a per student basis. To offset its start-up costs, Great Plains IDEA secured numerous grants, including those from the United States Department of Agriculture (USDA) and the Department of Education's Fund for the Improvement of Post-Secondary Education (FIPSE). It did not charge an initial membership fee or expect up-front monetary contributions from its members.

Setting Parameters

Determining boundaries between the shared operations and individual partner prerogative is accomplished through consensus and forethought and also through trial and error. Determining an alliance task from an individual partner responsibility proved challenging for Great Plains IDEA. It figured this out for the most part by muddling through. Kansas State's Great Plain IDEA Program Coordinator Dawn Anderson said,

> We talked about stuff like promotion and tenure, evaluation, and how the money should be distributed within the institution. These issues were just talked about over and over, almost ad-nauseam, and each institution was so different and there was never any consensus.... Finally, we realized that there are just some things that the alliance just can't do and we had to make that clear and then to realize that was a real accomplishment.

In determining which decisions should be made collectively and which ones are institutional responsibilities, some clear lessons emerged. The first is, attempt to determine criteria to differentiate between institutional and alliance decisions. The leadership of Great Plains IDEA decided to avoid decisions that would require partner institutions to make significant changes in their policies. Some of the issues it considered, but then backed away from, included the use of the GRE for admission and common requirements for a thesis or comprehensive examination. Some institutions had these policies in place, while others did not.

For those issues that required consistency, such as the number of credits required for a degree, the leaders chose to follow the partner's policy that was most strict and had the least amount of flexibility. They tried to avoid developing new alliance policies that might conflict with current institutional policies. Said Nebraska's Dean Marjorie Kostelnik,

> Whomever had the most stringent guideline for [policy] X, Y or Z was the guideline we followed. We didn't try to talk people out of [their policy].... We decided to use the most constraining, the most challenging set of rules.... Otherwise there would be people who would say, I can't compromise on this and when you don't have any room to compromise alliances fall apart.

Great Plains IDEA leaders also decided to focus their attention on programmatic issues and not on those concerned with institutional processes. David Hildebrand, graduate dean from South Dakota State, said,

> Programmatic decisions need to be alliance decisions. Process and procedure things should be a campus thing. How we process a graduate application or the procedure we use for enrolling students on campus [is an institutional decision]. There is no way that all the institutions could agree on the same process for this group of students if it is a different process than they use for all their other students.

Alliances also can choose to avoid making decisions about certain policies. Not every procedural "i" needs to be dotted or "t" crossed. For example, Great Plains

IDEA decided to avoid potentially divisive issues, such as how partners should allocate alliance revenue internally, or compensate and reward faculty teaching in the program. Institutions vary greatly on how these monies are distributed and how faculty members are paid for teaching distance education and/or graduate courses.

OneMBA did not struggle in the same ways. A set of factors may have contributed to this difference from the Great Plains IDEA experience. First, business school faculty and administrators tend to have come to consensus about the content of MBA programs. Second, the flexibility built into the design of OneMBA allowed individual partners to make curricular modifications when they felt strongly. Third, each partner had extensive experience with other partnerships so they were familiar with potential tensions between institutional and alliance boundaries. Fourth, executive board members spent significant time at the beginning of their effort defining what was an alliance issue and what was the responsibility of each institution (such as setting its own price, recruiting and compensating faculty, etc.). Finally, the process used to develop the program allowed different institutions the flexibility to participate in ways that were consistent with each institution's decision-making process.

In sum, CJV leaders need to create a focused, flexible, and multitiered infrastructure to coordinate joint alliance activities. Said David Ravenscraft, Associate Dean at UNC, about OneMBA, the intent of the champions was to design a structure that was decentralized, but "coordinated at the right levels." The chair of Great Plains IDEA, Virginia Moxley, Associate Dean at Kansas State, similarly reported, "One of the goals of this alliance is to have very little at the middle."

HOW IS EACH PARTNER'S SHARED GOVERNANCE PROCESS INVOLVED IN CURRICULAR JOINT VENTURES?

Successfully navigating each institution's program approval process is one of the more significant governance challenges of interinstitutional programs. Approval for new academic programs can be a multistep process involving peer faculty review (sometimes at multiple levels), administrative review, and, frequently, system or board consideration. Program approval processes, even in the best of circumstances, can be onerous. The interinstitutional nature of these programs demanded not one, but multiple approvals simultaneously at participating universities.

The lesson is, lay the groundwork for campus approval early. Alliance leaders need to be intentional about seeking approval through a process that involves both faculty and administrative reviews, and sometimes trustee or state coordinating board approval. Great Plains IDEA leaders were careful because the joint programs were highly innovative on most partner campuses. They were online, interdisciplinary, interinstitutional, and graduate. GP IDEA leaders spent significant time keeping a variety of key decision makers well informed about their intentions, the program designs, and the rationale for offering programs such as these collaboratively. Said Associate Dean Antigone Kotsiopulos from Colorado State, "It is a little tricky to come home with the very first program and try to explain it to your colleagues."

Effective strategies to gain support consist of holding ongoing meetings, both formal and informal, with key decision makers, preparing documents, and addressing concerns of key governance bodies well in advance. The specifics of how leaders did this on each campus varied as the stakeholders and decision processes differed from one partner institution to the next. The alliances relied heavily on campus leaders who knew their own institutions well, including the potential political minefields, the formal and informal opinion leaders, and relevant past histories with program approval. Once faculty and administrative decision makers were comfortable with the novelty of the program, they tended to be supportive. The challenges that surfaced tended to focus on the fact that the proposed program was offered through distance learning or that it was interdisciplinary and not on its interinstitutional nature.

For OneMBA, the approval processes also differed by institution, but they occurred smoothly. For example, at the University of North Carolina, the business school faculty, which have the power to veto such a program, were kept well aware of the program and its progression, and for the most part, they approved. Said David Ravenscraft, associate dean,

> We really didn't have much resistance from our faculty. I heard from some faculty that we were crazy, that it would be difficult to coordinate that many schools, but we didn't get resistance. It was the power of the idea that helped convince the faculty that this is [the best way to go].

The associate dean, responsible for UNC's involvement in OneMBA, kept key opinion leaders informed. People were well aware of what the program was attempting to do and why it was important to the school. He also had the full support of the dean from the beginning. Said Program Manager Penny Oslund of UNC,

> We made a number of presentations. We answered a lot of questions. We did a lot of hallway work.... I think the faculty had enough respect for David and the fact that we had a really strong executive MBA program. They were not going to stand in the way, although they were going to continue to express their opinions.

Approval was more difficult, for example, at the Chinese University of Hong Kong (CUHK), which required multiple levels that many noted is expected in a Chinese bureaucracy. One area that was particularly troublesome was OneMBA's nontraditional course schedule, which slowed the approval process at CUHK, so much so that the first year it had to adhere to its traditional MBA schedule. The Rotterdam School of Management (RSM), in contrast, had little trouble because of its flat organizational structure. RSM's Associate Dean Mike Page said,

> We did not have to go through a traditional university approval by Council and Senate, etc.... We presented the idea to the faculty committee, we sought their counsel on how we should structure it, and [addressed] the questions and concerns they had about it. The flat structure is such that these sorts of conversations happen on an ongoing basis, rather than a situation [where] a faculty board meets on the third Thursday of every third semester kind of thing.

For some institutions, such as UNC and Fundação Getulio Vargas (FGV), their current executive MBA program offerings facilitated OneMBA's approval because nontraditional programs were already an accepted part of the curriculum. Said UNC's Oslund,

> If this had been a totally new concept run out of another area there would have been a lot more hurdles.... Our other two [EMBA] programs helped plow the way, which might be why it didn't look like there were such great [internal] hurdles.

DO CJVS COMPLICATE INSTITUTIONAL SHARED GOVERNANCE? DOES SHARED GOVERNANCE COMPLICATE CJVS?

The answer to these questions is that there can be relatively little complication of one for the other. In these two cases, shared governance worked well as did alliance governance, and each did so in its separate spheres. Because of the complexities of CJVs, and the potential conflicts over curricular decisions, one might speculate that CJVs could be challenging for institutional governance. One also might suspect that campus shared governance can complicate interinstitutional program development. A single program, because it is shared jointly, must adhere to multiple governance processes that might yield competing amendments before approval. The politics of a single campus might derail an otherwise worthy project that spans many institutions. The multiple processes might be so cumbersome that CJVs wither on the vine.

However, neither OneMBA or Great Plains IDEA experienced these problems. Alliance decisions for the most part were distinct from campus governance decisions. The complexity created by CJV decisions was resolved within each alliance, and did not spill into individual campus decision-making processes. CJV leaders created legitimate decision-making processes within each alliance (some intentionally, others through trial and error) and built respectful yet firm firewalls between alliance activities and institutional decision processes. They respected campus processes and knew when institutional governance processes were needed to advance the interinstitutional program. Institutions differentiated alliance decisions from institutional decisions and CJV leaders served as gatekeepers. When CJV leaders needed to seek formal campus approval, they did so through established campus governance processes in much the same way they would if they were seeking approval for a new program offered solely by their institution.

MAKING SENSE OF INTERINSTITUTIONAL ACADEMIC DECISIONS

These two cases demonstrate that in curricular joint ventures two types of academic decision making occur—institutional, which is involved primarily in the approval process, and alliance, which is a joint partner responsibility—and campus leaders can successfully manage each and bridge both processes as necessary. However, institutional leaders frequently are concerned with how to make academic decision making run more smoothly, be more efficient, and be less contentious. These two cases do not suggest that the decisions related to CJVs will always be smooth, as academic decision making, even at a single institution, can be unpredictable, fickle, forthright, and demanding. That said, what insights do these two examples offer?

First, the CJVs had goals viewed as agreeable by campus decision makers (of all types). Faculty as well as administrators saw the CJVs as win-win situations. In the case of Great Plains IDEA, its explicit purpose was to develop graduate programs that a single institution would be unable to offer because of limited expertise and capacity. It allowed faculty with specialties in family financial planning, youth development, and gerontology to connect with a group of scholarly peers from other institutions and develop a new, innovative graduate program. As for OneMBA, this program was a highly visible effort to create an MBA program that was superior (in the minds of the participants) to the international executive education model used by key "industry leaders" such as Harvard, Columbia, and the London School of Economics. Because the five partners were all well respected, association with each other and the alliance lent additional prestige that helped make the efforts more acceptable. Said Julie Yu, CUHK's representative,

> The Chinese University's MBA programs are focused upon four core values: globalization, relevance, innovation and quality.... It is obvious that our core values are very well expressed in this particular program, so OneMBA is a great fit for us.

Second, potential naysayers did not view the programs as competing for financial resources with their own priorities. Great Plains IDEA found external support to launch and initiate the alliance. OneMBA, even though it required investment from each school, was able to show its faculty decision makers that the program's immediate value outweighed its costs. Although some grumbling did occur at UNC, for example, by faculty wanting support for their own programs, this was not substantial enough to create problems for OneMBA. As a person from OneMBA said, "even faculty can recognize a really good idea."

Third, the alliances were led by experienced advocates, who adhered to established campus governance paths. In campus governance, legitimate processes in which actors adhere to expected processes is key (Birnbaum, 1988; Eckel, 2003 also see Chapter 5). The people responsible for leading the efforts knew how decision making worked at their respective campuses. They were seasoned and understood the types of issues and processes that could be potential stumbling blocks.

They knew at what point and in what way they should involve key institutional stakeholders. Said Robert Sullivan, former dean at UNC about OneMBA's lead champion David Ravenscraft,

> He has the respect and a very good rapport with the faculty and he is faculty, and that played a very important role with its [success]. Because he was accepted, he was credible, he was liked. You could have an even better model, but have somebody who doesn't have that credibility with the faculty and that initiative would go down the tubes.

In both cases, alliance leaders were able to balance the tension inherent in alliance structures between institutional autonomy and collective decision making. The tension between these two elements often leads to unclear alliance structures (Spekman, Forbes, Isabella, & MacAvoy, 1998).

Fourth, the CJV leadership identified workable guiding principles, sought agreement on them, and stuck to them. The fact that both CJVs articulated guiding principles and that they were similar in many ways is worth noting. These principles were active documents, and used continually to inform decisions and reiterate priorities and purposes. They set the ground rules for alliance behavior and acted as a social contract for the group.

Finally, the partners were well known to one another. One factor frequently mentioned by those interviewed about Great Plains IDEA was the familiarity among partners, which can breed trust (Gulati, 1995)—a necessary element in forging and sustaining successful alliances (Lewis, 1999; Ring & Van de Ven, 1994). Because they were familiar with one another, the participants had a good sense of what was "do-able" together and at each individual partner. Said Nebraska's Kostelnik,

> You have to know your partners. You can't just walk in randomly and say let's take these ten schools. There has to be a real reason for the partner to be there. You have common interests. Some of you have worked together before. You have to have some history, or at least some members that have history. You are going to rely upon that history to carry you through some tough times. You don't just look them up in the phone book.

OneMBA also built itself upon familiar ground. To identify institutions with which to partner, UNC looked to its long-standing relationships with foreign business schools. For example, the then-dean of the CUHK was a former doctoral advisee of the then–UNC Dean Robert Sullivan. Sullivan had a long-standing relationship with EGADE, helping them to establish a doctoral program a decade previous. The faculty member responsible for many of EGADE's international relationships, Alejandro Ruelas-Gossi, was a UNC graduate. FGV and UNC also had collaborated on undergraduate programs. Because of the familiarity of partners, alliance participants did not have to spend time first getting to know one another. They were confident that they could work through disagreements, and they expected that they could minimize, if not avoid, procedural or cultural surprises that might surface through various decision-making processes.

In closing, one might be tempted to conclude that the lack of conflict suggests that campus governance did not play a significant role in interinstitutional decision making. That would be a misguided assumption. Campus governance did make important contributions to curricular joint ventures in these two cases. That is, it worked just fine.

NOTE

This chapter is based on the American Council on Education (ACE)'s Changing Enterprise Project (http://www.acenet.edu/programs/change-enterprise), which is supported by contributions from Accenture, The Goldman Sachs Foundation, and Peterson's, a Thomson Learning Company. An earlier draft of this paper was given at the Annual Meeting of the Assocation for the Study of Higher Education (ASHE), November 2003, Portland, OR. The author can be reached at the American Council on Education, One Dupont Circle, NW, Washington, DC 20036 or Peter_Eckel@ace.nche.edu.

REFERENCES

American Council on Education (2004). *Shifting ground: Autonomy, accountability and privatization in public higher education.* (The Changing Relationship Between States and Their Institutions Series, Paper 1). Washington DC: American Council on Education.

American Association of University Professors (2001). *Policy documents and reports* (9th ed.). Washington, DC: Author.

Bailey, D., & McNally Koney, K (2000). *Strategic alliances among health and human services organizations: From affiliations to consolidations.* Thousand Oaks, CA: Sage Publications.

Barringer, B. R., & Harrison, J. S. (2000). Walking a tightrope: Creating value through interorganizational relationships. *Journal of Management, 26*(3), 367–403.

Birnbaum, R. (1988). *How colleges work: The cybernetics of academic organization and leadership.* San Francisco: Jossey-Bass.

Bok, D. (2003). *Universities in the marketplace: The commercialization of higher education.* Princeton, NJ: Princeton University Press.

Borys, B., & Jemison, D. B. (1989). Hybrid arrangements as strategic alliances: Theoretical issues in organizational combinations. *Academy of Management Review, 14,* 234–249.

Dotolo, L. G. & Strandness, J. T. (1999). *Best practices in higher education consortia: How institutions can work together. New Directions for Higher Education,* No. 106. San Francisco: Jossey-Bass.

Eckel, P. D. (2003). *Changing course: Making the hard decisions to eliminate academic programs.* Westport, CT: Praeger.

Eckel, P. D., Affolter-Caine, B., & Green, M. (2003). *New times, new strategies: Curricular joint ventures* (The Changing Enterprise Occasional Paper No. 2). Washington, DC: American Council on Education.

Eckel, P. D., Couturier, L. & Luu, D. T. (2005). Peering around the bend: The leadership challenges of privatization, accountability and market-based state policy. (The Changing Relationship Between States and Their Institutions Series, Paper 4). Washington DC: American Council on Education.

Gulati, R. (1995). Does familiarity breed trust? The implications of repeated ties for contractual choice in alliances. *The Academy of Management Journal, 38*(1), 85–112.

Gulati, R., & Singh, H. (1998). The architecture of cooperation: Managing coordination costs and appropriation concerns in strategic alliances. *Administrative Science Quarterly, 43*, 781–814.

Gumport, P. J. (1993). The contested terrain of academic program reduction. *Journal of Higher Education, 64*(3), 283–311.

Hagadoorn, J. (1993). Understanding the rationale of strategic partnering: Interorganizational modes of cooperation and sectoral differences. *Strategic Management Journal, 14*, 371–385.

Hardy, C. (1993). The cultural politics of retrenchment. *Planning for Higher Education, 21*(4), 16–20.

Hearn, J. C. (2004). *Diversifying campus revenue streams: Opportunities and risks.* Washington, DC: American Council on Education.

Kane, T. J., Orszag, P. R., & Gunter, D. L. (2003, May). *State fiscal constraints and higher education spending: The role of Medicaid and the business cycle.* Washington, DC: The Brookings Institution.

Lewis, J. D. (1999). *Trusted partners: How companies build mutual trust and win together.* New York: Free Press.

Marginson, S. (2004). Competition and markets in higher education: A "glonacal" analysis. *Policy Futures in Education, 2*(2), 175–244.

Newman, F., & Couturier, L. (2001). *The new competitive arena: Market forces invade the academy.* The Futures Project: Policy for Higher Education in a Changing World. Providence, RI: Brown University.

Newman, F., & Scurry, J. (2001). *Higher education in the digital rapids.* The Futures Project: Policy for Higher Education in a Changing World. Providence, RI: Brown University.

Oliver, C. (1990). Determinants of interorganizational relationships: Integration and future directions. *Academy of Management Review, 15*(2), 241–265.

Park, S. H., & Russo, M. V. (1996). When competition eclipses cooperation: An event history analysis of joint venture failure. *Management Science, 42*(6), 875–890.

Ring, P. S., & Van de Ven, A. H. (1994). Developmental processes of cooperative interorganizational relationships. *Academy of Management Review, 19*, 90–118.

Rondinelli, D. A., & London, T. (2001). *Partnering for sustainability: Managing nonprofit organization-corporate environmental alliances.* Washington, DC: The Aspen Institute.

Spekman, R. E., Forbes, T. M., Isabella, L. A., & MacAvoy, T. C. (1998). Alliance management: A view from the past and look to the future. *Journal of Management Studies, 35*(6), 747–772.

Whealler Johnson S., & Noftsinger, J. B. (2004, July/August). Getting a grip on strategic alliances. *Trusteeship, 12*(4), 15–19.

Whetten, D. A. (1981). Interorganizational relations: A review of the field. *Journal of Higher Education, 52*, 1–28.

CHAPTER

The Tenuous Legitimacy of Ad Hoc Decision-Making Committees

Matthew Hartley and Simi R. Wilhelm Shah[1]
The University of Pennsylvania

INTRODUCTION

In a recent article in *The Chronicle of Higher Education* (Goldstein, 2005), a department chair offers a whimsical account of cleaning out his predecessor's old files. Sifting through various strata of documents, he finds correspondence from a "dean's task force on you-fill-in-the-blank": He discards it. The lighthearted allusion points to the ubiquity of ad hoc decision-making structures at colleges and universities, as perennial and ephemeral as the daisy. A host of standing committees (e.g., the curriculum committee or board subcommittee on endowment management) handles the bulk of day-to-day business under the system of collegial governance, which is embraced (to a greater or lesser extent) at the majority of colleges and universities. However, circumstances sometimes call for the establishment of special committees or task forces. These are parallel governance structures. They function independently of existing governance processes and procedures and their influence can be substantial.

Over the past two decades, academic leaders have increasingly made use of ad hoc committees for the purpose of advancing broad-based institutional change. In the mid-1980s, George Keller (1983) observed that "Joint Big Decision Committees" (JBDC) were "springing up like mushrooms" (p. 61). Kathleen Corak (1992) examined 30 JBDCs in the early 1990s. She found that institutions formed these decision-making structures for three principal reasons—they were a means of addressing academic issues that involved multiple schools or departments. The committees were efficient because they were not preoccupied with day-to-day matters, as standing committees are, and therefore, could focus their energies on the larger institutional issues at hand. They were also a useful strategy for securing broad-based political support for new initiatives.

A similar set of benefits is referenced in the organizational change literature. Jeanie Daniel Duck (1993) has advocated the use of Transition Management Teams (TMTs) in corporate restructuring to promote communication, assist in planning, and to coordinate broad-based initiatives. John Kotter's (1996) comprehensive research on corporate change found that a central feature of successful efforts is the presence of a "guiding coalition"—a group of well-respected and powerful individuals who are committed to conceptualizing, overseeing, and sustaining change. Like Keller, Kotter underscores the importance of involving multiple constituents in the change effort:

> Because major change is so difficult to accomplish, a powerful force is required to sustain the process. No one individual, even a monarch-like CEO, is ever able to develop the right vision, communicate it to large numbers of people, eliminate all key obstacles, generate short-term wins, lead and manage dozens of change projects, and anchor new approaches deep in the organization's culture…. A strong guiding coalition is always needed. (p. 52)

The use of ad hoc decision-making committees at colleges and universities in order to promote significant organizational change appears to be growing. In 1999, the Institute for Research on Higher Education (IRHE) at the University of Pennsylvania surveyed senior academic officers (provost or vice president for academic affairs) from 100 colleges and universities. Fifty-five percent responded that their institutions had recently created ad-hoc decision-making committees. Whether these committees are variations of the JBDC or a distinct structural form is unclear. What is certain is that many colleges and universities are experimenting with governance structures in an effort to adapt more quickly to an environment characterized by intense competition, shifting demographics, and uncertainty over funding. A decade ago, David Breneman (1995), dean of the Curry School of Education at the University of Virginia and a former college president, observed: "The collegial nature of most colleges and universities, emphasizing consultation and shared decision making, seems poorly suited to the sorts of wrenching challenges that lie ahead." Many senior administrators would concur with his prescient remark today.

Despite the prevalence and evident utility of ad hoc decision-making committees, a rather fundamental question has yet to be adequately addressed: Are they a legitimate form of academic governance? Does their independence from existing governance structures (the very characteristic that produces greater efficiency of action) enable them to function as the academic equivalent of the smoke-filled back room? Are handpicked partisans conspiring behind a façade of impartiality and independence? Or are there ways of ensuring the legitimacy of these useful structures? This chapter describes and examines the experiences of four ad hoc decision-making committees and identifies the factors that that positively or negatively influence perceptions of their legitimacy as alternative governance structures.

In conducting this research, our goals were threefold: to better understand why ad hoc decision-making committees (hereafter referred to simply as "committees") were chosen over existing governance channels, to describe their work, and to develop a clearer sense of the factors that influence the perceived legitimacy of these structures. Our sampling strategy entailed searching *The Chronicle of Higher Education* Web site and the Internet more generally, using terms such as "task force." We developed a list of 24 examples from four-year, accredited colleges and universities. After reviewing documents from their Web sites, we conducted pilot telephone interviews with people at the 12 institutions that seemed most promising. Finally, we settled on four information-rich cases (Patton, 1990) using the following criteria: All four sites established special committees whose purpose was to strengthen and reaffirm the academic mission of their institution. Although several of the interventions focused on cocurricular issues—student experience outside of the classroom—their intent was to positively influence the academic enterprise. The committees involved multiple constituents (e.g., staff, faculty, board members) and therefore were addressing issues of campus-wide importance. Finally, to ensure memories were still fresh, we selected sites where the committees had completed their work in the past five years.

We conducted in-depth, semistructured interviews (Rubin & Rubin, 1995) with seven people to learn the rationale for the creation of the committee, how its members were selected, how it structured its work, and to get a sense of the perceived outcome of its efforts. Participants were assured anonymity to encourage greater candor (Glesne & Peshkin, 1992). Participants and institutions are disguised in the cases. We reviewed institutional documents (e.g., committee charges, memoranda, reports outlining recommendations, institutional press releases). The data were coded separately by each investigator and then compared and contextualized collaboratively (Maxwell, 1996).

LEGITIMACY AS A KEY INDICATOR OF GOOD GOVERNANCE

Colleges and universities have somewhat different sets of expectations and customs in their governance procedures. One campus might expect the president to appoint members of a task force where at another this might be viewed as a gross violation of the faculty's right to select (or at least recommend) its own representatives. Therefore the surest way of assessing "good governance" is to ask individuals who understand the prevailing norms. We found that people's perceptions of the legitimacy of the committees we studied were an important means of assessing their efficacy. In fact, effective and efficient decision making is only possible when people believe that the established institutional processes are well reasoned and fair (Brockner, Chen, Mannix, Leung, & Skarlicki, 2000; Greenberg, 1990; Lind & Tyler, 1988) because people spend more time on-task and the organization expends less energy countering naysayers.

Establishing legitimacy is particularly important at collegial institutions that operate under the precepts of shared governance, that is, where each constituent group is assumed to have a role in institutional decision making (contingent on the issue at hand—adjusting a school's general education offerings would not occasion the participation of the board, for example). Colleges and universities resist the hierarchical coordination and control associated with corporate management (Birnbaum, 1988). A key reason is that the core activities of a college or university—teaching and research—require a group of professionals with highly specialized training who operate with considerable autonomy. Thus, power is diffuse in such organizations (Weick, 1976)—no individual or group can force the compliance of another. The faculty cannot compel the board to raise funds for a new science building. Neither can the administration require the faculty to engage in extensive curricular reform. Like participants in a three-legged race, the various constituents depend on one another to take even a step forward. Success requires excellent communication, good will, and trust.

Effective academic leaders are those whose efforts are seen as legitimate by the other constituents. Indeed, one of the most comprehensive studies of the college presidency found that effective long-term presidents were viewed as "honoring and working within established governance structures, accepting faculty participation in decision making, and being concerned with process" (Birnbaum, 1992). This calls for careful attention to *how* decisions are made. It is not only important to make the right decision but to have it made in the right way.

The cases described below point to several factors that influenced the perceived legitimacy of the committees' work. Not surprisingly, the first is the adequate representation of constituents, an issue that has served as the focus of several normative statements on academic governance (American Association of University Professors, 1995; Association of Governing Boards of Universities and Colleges, 1998). But the cases also reveal much about the quality of participation. The robust literature on procedural justice in organizations[2] describes several factors that shape perceptions of legitimacy in decision making. The earliest conception of organizational justice, equity theory, emphasized self-interest—"Am I getting my fair share?" (Adams, 1963). Thibaut and Walker (1975) later observed that people determine fairness by asking two key questions: Is the process used to make the decisions sensible and clear (termed "process control"), and is it possible for me to influence the outcome ("decision control") (Greenberg, 1990, p. 402)?

The cases that follow provide useful illustrations of how procedural legitimacy is advanced or thwarted, which are discussed in detail in our subsequent analysis. To facilitate comparisons between the cases, we invite readers to consider the following three questions as they review them:

1. What process did the committee establish to engage in decision making? (e.g., How often did the committee meet? How was the membership of the committee constituted?)

2. What (and who) influenced the decision making? (e.g., Who was consulted and how?)

3. What was the reaction to the eventual recommendations of the committee and what contributed to that response?

FOUR ILLUSTRATIVE EXAMPLES
Greenlawn University[3]

Greenlawn University is a highly selective, residential, private liberal arts college in a rural area. The university has a long-established Greek-letter system and fraternities and sororities dominate student social life. They have also been something of a thorn in the administration's side, producing a steady stream of incident reports and repeated alcohol violations. A decade earlier, Greenlawn's president established a task force whose eventual recommendations called for radical reform. Though endorsed by the board and the faculty, no noticeable change in policies or procedures followed. Then, a serious injury and three student deaths occurred in rapid succession. Some linked the tragedies to social activities within the Greek system. This prompted a group of board members to act.

The board members requested an immediate meeting with Greenlawn's president and the dean of students. The following week, the chair of the board announced to the faculty, staff, and students that the trustees were commissioning a "task force" to conduct a comprehensive review of the student residential life system and to make recommendations for significantly restructuring it. One staff member described the board's actions as an indication of growing dissatisfaction with the president. "This issue was just too important to leave alone and it became clear, to the trustees at least, that they needed to step in because of an absence of leadership." Soon afterward, the president announced his intention to retire.

A board member was made chair of the new Residential Life Committee (RLC) and she (in consultation with the dean of students) selected a group of 26 trustees, students, and staff and faculty members to serve on it. The group met in closed sessions in order to allow for "difficult and frank" conversations. Subcommittees were formed to gather information on campus and to visit four peer institutions whose residential life systems were considered exemplary. The committee's work extended over a three-year period.

The initial stated goal of the committee—to reinvigorate Greenlawn's residential life system and to improve cocurricular programming for students—was greeted favorably by the university community (based on the accounts of institutional members and editorials in the student newspaper). Over time, however, speculation over the work of the committee became the grist for an increasingly ugly rumor mill. Leaders of the Pan-Hellenic Society (the elected officers of the Greek chapters on campus) began expressing concerns that the RLC was a clandestine effort to dismantle the Greek system. Committee members were subject to intense lobbying that at times bordered on harassment. A student member later reported significant social stigmatization as a result of his participation. An administrator who served on the committee remarked:

> There was a lot of mistrust and suspicion of the committee ... before the
> recommendations came out. There was a veil of mystery around the task force

which was unfortunate. There was a lot of negative energy towards the group before anyone knew any of the outcomes.

When the initial report of the committee was delivered to the college's new president, it recommended sweeping changes to the residential life system, including far greater policing of and sharply curtailed autonomy for the Greek houses. It argued for the establishment of a comprehensive "alternative" residential life program, including an expansion of theme housing and more apartment-style housing options for students. Although Greenlawn had always allowed students to live off campus, the report recommended drastically reducing or even eliminating this option so the student affairs division could more closely control students' campus life experience.

Greenlawn's new president immediately sent copies of the report to the entire board, to a select group of alumni leaders, and made multiple copies available in the campus library for students and others to review. The document evoked strong responses. Many students (even those not affiliated with fraternities or sororities) protested the recommendations. The Pan-Hellenic Society stated that the proposal infantilized students and argued that if promoting leadership was a central tenet of an excellent liberal arts education, the recommended changes eliminated a primary means of cultivating such talents. It went on to declare the entire process "a sham" and condemned the document as a direct assault on Greek life.

A number of alumni, and even a few board members, contacted the president and expressed their strong disapproval of what seemed to them a heavy-handed course of action. There were numerous appeals to the board and to the president for a more measured level of change. The president asked the RLC to carefully consider these responses.

The revised (and final) report of the RLC softened much of its language. Although the report still called for careful oversight of fraternities and sororities, the autonomy of the Greek houses was to remain untouched. Rather than calling for the creation of an alternative social life system, the report instead advocated the allocation of resources in order to enhance and expand the range of social options for students. The report also advocated a slight reduction in the number of students living off campus.

Comments
Greenlawn's RLC began with the endorsement of the university's board and was established as a large (26-member), broadly representative group drawn from multiple constituents. Its initial charge was widely endorsed. However, the committee's closed sessions and the absence of any venue for campus members to directly influence discussions (and therefore the decision making) eroded its legitimacy. The decision not to engage the larger campus community in deliberations and to then recommend sweeping changes created an environment conducive to cynicism and dissent.

Mountain University

Mountain University is a highly selective, prestigious, private research university nestled in the foothills of a rural area. Mountain's alumni are fiercely loyal (as evidenced by the institution's healthy endowment) and its alumni association is quite active. Soon after his inauguration, Mountain's new president surprised many by announcing that the out-of-classroom experience at Mountain needed to undergo radical change. Surveys over the past several years had found that although students were extremely satisfied with Mountain's academic programs, they were equally dissatisfied with the cocurriculum. The overall campus life experience was lackluster. Social and cultural programming was limited, students complained.

Despite these findings (or perhaps because they were unaware of them), many felt that the president's conclusions were premature. A few senior faculty members openly questioned his judgment. A flood of e-mails was sent to the president's office from all quarters counseling caution. The president's statement prompted a formal rebuke by the university's faculty senate for failing to adequately consult with them before advocating such a significant change. The statement ended somewhat ominously by indicating that the faculty would not support *any* initiative, no matter how laudatory, unless the faculty were properly consulted. One member of the administration admitted later that the initial call for change "was spun negatively and was a surprise to the larger community. [...] I don't know exactly what [the president] was thinking. I believe the reaction even startled him."

In an effort to diffuse the situation, the president and the board of trustees publicly announced the creation of a "blue ribbon committee" charged with weighing the impact of the president's proposed changes and to solicit recommendations about how they might best be implemented. One administrator noted that "the trustees at Mountain have always been hands-on. You could even say they have micromanaged policy decisions in the residential realm." In fact, within the past two years, the board had formed three separate committees to provide a "hands-on" response to perceived institutional problems regarding campus life.

The 16-member committee was led by two trustee chairs. Its membership, including undergraduate and graduate students, faculty, administrators, and alumni, was selected by the president. The group later spun off subgroups to focus on particular issues. The committee immediately began to conduct extensive interviews and to hold open forums in large and small settings to encourage discussion and debate. The alumni were also invited to participate. One member of the committee noted that the alumni had argued persuasively against some of the president's more radical early recommendations, stating that "[they] were very influential and leaned very hard on the president and the trustees with some measure of success."

Just about a year later, the group produced 11 recommendations, including a call for a more aggressive effort to address alcohol and drug abuse as well as the reorganization of the Greek-letter system. Although significant, the recommended changes were far more limited than those proposed by the president in his original announcement. A member of the committee observed: "The initial points were harsher than the eventual recommendations." The recommendations were formally accepted by the board and the faculty and implemented. Two years later, the results of these efforts are in the process of being systematically evaluated.

Comments

Mountain's committee faced a significant challenge early on. Although the committee's membership was broadly representative and though it enjoyed the endorsement of the board of trustees, the reason for creating the blue ribbon committee (at least as articulated by the president) was initially contested. Few concurred with the president's dire characterization of campus life. The committee navigated through these difficult waters by actively involving the campus community and the alumni in a series of discussions and debates about campus life through multiple venues (e.g., large meetings, small meetings, subcommittees.) Though somewhat measured, the final recommendations were widely accepted by the community.

Spirit University

Spirit University is a large public research university in a suburban setting with a widely recognized, successful athletic program. Two alcohol-related student deaths captured considerable media attention and generated intense pressure from external constituents. Parents and alumni expressed concerns about the safety of students and the adequacy of cocurricular programming. Members of the surrounding community noted an escalation in the number of incidents involving intoxicated students off campus. Town/gown relations had grown strained and many in the community openly questioned whether the university was willing to address problems related to student substance abuse.

At the behest of the president, the vice president for student affairs formed a committee to respond to the student deaths by reviewing all existing university policies and procedures pertaining to substance abuse. The vice president selected students, parents, faculty members, local police, members of the athletics department, and counseling, health, and campus safety officers to serve on the 25-member committee.

During its initial meeting, the committee decided to focus its efforts on the university's alcohol policy and to suggest means for improving the coordination of its enforcement both on campus and off. Though most of its meetings were scheduled privately and therefore not open to the public, the members organized a series of forums during which they described the committee's work and solicited feedback on its work and the alcohol policy in general. The group also created several small working groups that researched policies on other campuses. Ultimately, the committee advanced 28 recommendations to the vice president. She, in turn, invited reactions by the campus community. Some students and alumni lobbied to change a few of the proposed restrictions regarding when and how student organizations could serve alcohol. These were amended. Ultimately, all 28 recommendations were acted on, with a number sent to various standing university and board committees for approval. A committee member concluded:

> The Greeks would say that the process was a success because they lobbied for some changes and got them. The university would agree because the recommendations were stricter than they were before, although the initial recommendations were stricter, then they came down a bit. But the university would be pleased overall.

Comments

Spirit's committee derived its initial charge from the president in the aftermath of a tragedy. There was a clear consensus that change needed to occur. Although the committee eventually focused on an issue that was the purview of student affairs, the vice president elected to draw broadly for its membership. The composition of the committee reflected the range of constituencies concerned about substance abuse (e.g., faculty, administrators, parents, community members). It also indicated the committee's desire to open itself to influence by multiple groups. Its subsequent decision to constrain its charge (that is, to focus on alcohol policies rather than all issues associated with substance abuse), its use of open meetings, its careful gathering of data from other institutions, and the vice president's request for responses to the committee's findings all helped establish the legitimacy of the final recommendations.

Great State University

Great State University is a mid-sized public research university. In recent years, the president, the board of regents, and the faculty had grown increasingly concerned about the university's academic standing and the perceived decline in the caliber of admitted students. There were also concerns that many of Great State's most academically talented students were transferring out by the end of the sophomore year. The president concluded that significant institutional change was needed. She had recently championed the decision to go to Division 1 in athletics in hopes of engendering a sense of excitement and pride in the institution. However, in her view, a far more comprehensive institutional initiative was warranted.

The president asked a well-respected, senior professor to form a committee comprised of 17 faculty, students, and staff members to examine institutional support for undergraduate learning. A member of the president's staff also sat on the committee. The president announced (quite publicly) that the committee would be completely autonomous and that their findings would be the result of an impartial investigation. She encouraged them to be creative and impartial and to indicate what they viewed as the optimal solution for the university.

During their first few meetings, however, the president's representative to the committee began presenting a series of proposals for improving undergraduate learning. Some members of the committee got the distinct impression that the representative was simply serving as a mouthpiece for the president. One faculty member recalled, "I got the distinct impression from the president's representative that the president wanted an honors program. But she did not want to make the decision herself unilaterally, perhaps because she wanted to avoid any controversy."

The committee met for a year in private. When its initial recommendations were formed, it held several focus groups in order to gauge the response of the community to various potential initiatives.

Ultimately, the committee report proposed three recommendations for the president's approval: First, to institute an honors college specifically aimed at serving academically talented students; second, to establish a more deliberate link between academics and the residential life program (e.g., faculty in residence programs, the establishment of pilot learning communities); and, finally, to encourage more interdisciplinary work through an "integrated curriculum." Initially, there was grumbling among the faculty about not being adequately consulted. Some felt the proposed changes constituted an unfair indictment of the existing academic program. The committee chair, however, noted that the committee had held focus groups and the proposals were being presented to the university's various standing committees for discussion.

Comments

Great State's committee was charged with addressing a central academic issue—institutional support for undergraduate learning. The president publicly asked the committee to reexamine the university's current efforts and to recommend reform. The committee's initial legitimacy was aided by the excellent reputation of its faculty chairperson. However, the response to the committee's work revealed that not all faculty members felt that significant change was warranted. There were also concerns about adequate consultation. Although its members represented various constituent groups, its comparatively small size (10 members) meant that each constituent group—including the faculty—had few representatives in total. Further, though the committee did seek feedback, it did so through the rather limited (and somewhat scripted) use of focus groups. Finally, the actions of the president's representative caused at least some members to call into question the committee's independence.

ANALYSIS AND FINDINGS

In the analysis that follows, we begin by outlining the benefits and the limitations of these ad hoc decision-making committees and then go on to describe the factors that influenced their perceived legitimacy.

The Benefits of Ad Hoc Decision-Making Committees

These cases suggest that these committees can potentially serve many useful purposes. First, they are efficient. Rather than asking multiple standing committees to engage in duplicative efforts, ad hoc decision-making committees bring together a select group of knowledgeable individuals to look closely at an issue, to weigh possible responses, and to make recommendations.

Second, they are an effective strategy for making decisions. The membership of the group can be tailored to suit the interests of various groups and to ensure that people with particular kinds of expertise (e.g., an understanding of the organization, a particular expertise regarding the topic at hand) are involved. Decision-making theorists note that committees comprised of people with disparate positions and perspectives tend to consider a wider range of potential organizational responses and tend to produce better decisions (Garvin & Roberto, 2001; Hammond, Keeney, & Raiffa, 2001). A broader range of participants also can prevent narrow interests or perspectives from prevailing. We were encouraged in these cases by the judicious inclusion of constituents usually missing from university committees (e.g., alumni, parents, community members) when dealing with issues impacting these groups.

Third, committees allow people from across the institution to collectively engage in sensemaking (Weick, 1995). Colleges and universities are complex and compartmentalized organizations. The perspective of individuals tends to be constrained by their positions in the organization. The shocked response to Mountain's president's bold call for change is an indication that different groups held vastly different perspectives about the university's situation. Happily, the committee's subsequent efforts at reaching out to the wider campus community ultimately helped forge a consensus that change was, in fact, warranted. Their work underscores the potential for such committees to help the entire campus develop a shared understanding of the challenges the institution faces and the opportunities that are available.

Mountain's experience also points to a fourth benefit of ad hoc committees. If they are diverse and staffed by individuals with significant influence in the organization, they can serve as a "guiding coalition" (Kotter, 1996)—a core group of supporters who can champion the effort. Mountain's committee's decision to create public forums for debate increased the base of support for the change effort and enabled the committee to understand and respond to the concerns of those ambivalent about change.

Fifth, ad hoc committees are a means of powerfully communicating institutional responsiveness to a particular issue—elevating its level of importance. A committee member at Spirit University explains:

> We elevated the problem [of substance abuse] to the status that few things are ever elevated, which showed that we think this is really important. You just don't communicate that when a vice president writes a policy in her office—even if the results are the same. Our most powerful changes have

resulted from the public perception. The task force was a way to bring previously fragmented and inconsistent policies together and to bring outside
voices inside.

By establishing a high-profile committee, institutional leaders at Spirit signaled to
parents, alumni, and the community that they understood a problem existed and
were willing to invest considerable time and effort on its resolution. Further, the
inclusion of community members and parents on the committee suggested that
the effort would not be a whitewash.

LIMITATIONS AND LIABILITIES

There are, of course, a number of potential limitations and liabilities to using
ad hoc decision-making committees.

Corak (1992) and others have argued that ad hoc committees are efficient
because they are not distracted by routine, run-of-the-mill decision making that
encumbers many standing committees. This seems sensible. However, we found no
evidence in these four cases that decisions were arrived at with any greater speed.
Indeed, the faculty chair at Great State grumbled that the "the president wanted
answers *too soon*" and the committee refused to be rushed and proceeded at a
deliberate and measured pace while generating its recommendations. Rather than
producing faster decisions, the cases suggest that the committees at best arguably
allowed for a more thorough and sustained examination of the issue at hand.

Second, if relations between groups are strained, elevating an issue by establishing a high-profile presidential or board committee can be a liability. Great State's
committee was able to go quietly about its business with virtually no resistance
precisely because people did not link the initiative to the president (which was
her reason for forming the group.) A high-profile committee is more likely to face
scrutiny by naysayers. It also runs the risk of providing grist for the rumor mill if it
is not vigilant in its efforts at communicating with the larger campus community,
as Greenlawn's RLC discovered.

A final liability of these committees is their potential for being the objects of
political manipulation. Some members of Great State's committee viewed the
array of proposals presented by the president's representative in committee meetings as a rather transparent attempt by the administration to shape the committee's findings. Although there is nothing wrong with the president of a university
voicing his or her opinion, this president's very public declarations about the
committee's independence and impartiality made her representative's actions
(and by extension the president's) appear disingenuous.

EARNING LEGITIMACY

The legitimacy of organizational structures is in the eye of the beholders.
Individual campuses may have decidedly different views on what role various

constituents may play in academic governance. However, these cases point to a number of factors that influence perceptions of legitimacy. Ad hoc committees are more likely to be viewed as legitimate when the process of decision making is clearly articulated, seems rational to organizational members, and is transparent (process control), and when various constituents believe that the decision-making process is actually open to influence (decision control) (Thibaut & Walker, 1975).

Process Control

In these cases, the composition of the committees clearly contributed to their perceived legitimacy. Each committee had broad representation. This seems to have been a normative response—having multiple constituents was simply "the way things are done here." The presence of certain individuals also positively influenced perceptions of the committee. For example, having a board member chair a committee signals a very high level of institutional commitment to the issue at hand. At Great State, the presence of an esteemed senior colleague bolstered the committee's legitimacy in the eyes of the faculty.

The data seem to suggest that the size of the committee may influence whether people feel the decision-making process is designed in a way that will adequately represent them. A committee with 10 members arguably has a lesser claim on being representative than one with three times that number. Size is relevant for another reason: Although a larger group may be more inefficient (e.g., difficulties in scheduling, a revolving carousel of members), it is also less likely to be viewed as a collection of "yes men" than a small one. A larger size may contribute to the perceived impartiality of the group.

How representatives are selected warrants special consideration. In these cases, the members were handpicked by the institutional leader(s) forming the committees. There are sensible reasons for this practice. A leader may have special insights into people who will work well together or who have various kinds of expertise. The leader may use the opportunity to cultivate new faculty or administrative leadership. The problem is that the potential exists for a leader to create a committee populated entirely by partisans. Not only is this unethical (if the committee is formed with the expressed intention of serving as an impartial decision-making body), it is also dangerous. A like-minded committee can fall into "groupthink" (Janis, 1972) and develop collective, ideologically driven rationalizations for a particular outcome rather than render a decision by carefully weighing the merits of disparate and even conflicting viewpoints. We found no evidence of "stacking the deck" in these cases. However, we were intrigued by the fact that not a single person interviewed had any idea what criteria were used to select committee members. As long as representation of key groups (e.g., faculty, students, administrators, alumni) was built into the structure, no one much cared *who* represented them. It may also be that individuals view representation as a rather limited means of influencing decision making itself. (The ineffectual lobbying effort of Greenlawn's RLC underscores this point.) Although having adequate representation is important, it is an insufficient means of establishing the legitimacy of the decision-making process.

A second aspect of process control is that the decision-making process must be transparent—open to scrutiny. Greenlawn's RLC chose to do nearly all its work in private because it was dealing with the extremely sensitive issue of restructuring or even possible eliminating the Greek system. However, this left the rest of the campus community blind to the committee's internal workings. In the absence of information, people naturally begin to speculate. At Greenlawn, this took the form of ugly rumors that fostered a persistent negative view of the committee long before it had made public any of its findings. Great State's use of focus groups also appears to have been perceived as an inadequate means of securing meaningful input. By contrast, Mountain and Spirit Universities' strategy, using a series of open and closed meetings, avoided that trap.

Allowing the work of the committee to be subject to ongoing scrutiny also serves as a check on the committee itself. It prevents the committee's line of reasoning from evolving so far beyond the prevailing views on campus that its ultimate conclusion (however well-reasoned) comes across as shockingly radical or pie-in-the-sky. The initial committee report at Greenlawn might have caused less shock if there had been consistent opportunities for others to see the evolving rationale for such significant change.

Decision Control

Individuals must not only feel that the process is reasonable and fair, they must also believe that it is open to external influence (Thibaut & Walker, 1975). These perceptions develop early on, even as the problem itself is being defined. At Spirit, the various committee members (e.g., parents and community members) initially had somewhat different definitions of the "problem" that needed to be addressed. Their initial task, therefore, was to delineate the scope of their work in a way that addressed all concerns. The reaction to Mountain's president's initial dire assessment of campus life suggests that many at the university either had experiences that contradicted his view or that they had not had adequate opportunity to weigh the evidence in order to arrive at the same conclusion as the president. Either way, the situation required a good deal of back-pedaling to placate a disgruntled faculty senate, among others. Although the president was still able to significantly shape the agenda of the committee (its charge was to review the impact of his proposed changes, not to construct an alternative plan), the decision to create a blue ribbon committee sent an important signal—that the president expected this to be a collaborative effort. That openness helped legitimize the committee's work.

The cases offer several examples of strategies committees used to seek the input of others. Spirit's committee had community representatives and parents serve as members. It also held a series of open forums in order to promote a lively give and take between campus and the wider community. Mountain and Greenlawn's reports promoted campus-wide discussions and both were subsequently amended in response to public input. However, we wonder if Greenlawn's committee had not waited to the very end of its deliberations to present its findings (for example, if it had floated a series of trial balloons) whether the campus' response to its report would have been more measured and perhaps the final document would not have had to be softened to such a large degree. In fact, discussing issues with the wider community would have served an important purpose. It would have allowed an informed committee to educate others about the imperative for significant change.

THOUGHTS FOR CAMPUS LEADERS

One conclusion of our investigation is that people do not examine the implications of their governance processes. Indeed, several participants in this research had a difficult time even grasping the import of the study, saying, essentially, "Why does it matter whether we use these committees or not and who's involved, as long as a decision is reached that everyone can accept?" However, finding a solution to a vexing institutional issue that enjoys widespread support can be challenging. In fact, most significant decisions either leave a minority unhappy or represent a kind of compromise. This is the nature of governance. What makes the outcome palatable is the agreement that the process was fair and just.

Most of the people we interviewed viewed the ad hoc option as equivalent to (or even part of) the existing governance structure. That is simply not the case. In a real sense, they parallel (and even have the potential to circumvent) the governance system (Hartley, 2003). However, campus leaders can take an active role in ensuring that these structures will be accepted as legitimate. It is not only the right thing to do, but it also makes the likelihood that the decisions will be embraced and acted upon much greater. To that end, campus leaders forming such committees should consider the following:

- *How is the membership of the committee constituted?* Be clear about the criteria for inclusion on the committee. Consider soliciting nominations in order to identify individuals who are well respected. Leaders should ensure the membership is representative. Are all groups with a stake in the issue at the table? For certain issues, consideration should be given to inviting representatives of nontraditional constituents (e.g., parents, community members) to participate.

- *Will the committee be exposed to a variety of viewpoints?* The best decisions result from weighing multiple options. This is more likely when people with different viewpoints are involved. Though this can in part be accomplished by having a diversity of members, the committee should also make the collection of disparate (and even contradictory) views a central task. This can be done by interviewing people from across campus, structuring forums, and seeking the advice of people at institutions that have grappled with similar issues.

- *How transparent is the process of decision making?* The committee should structure opportunities to engage in conversations with the wider campus community on an ongoing basis. It should also develop a communication strategy and make use of various outlets (e.g., campus-wide e-mails, the campus press, the alumni magazine, the local paper) to describe its work. The work of various subcommittees and the committee as a whole should be summarized periodically and reported on.

- *What efforts have been made to ensure the committee is open to influence by others?* Focus groups and forums intended to convey information rather than foster dialogue do not allow for adequate input. Careful attention should be paid to structuring public meetings so they are productive. For example, various alternatives might be presented and comments invited. Whenever possible, the committee should indicate the evolution of its thought process through these events (e.g., indicate changes in text in successive drafts of reports).

- *Is dissent on the committee encouraged and protected?* It is impossible to stifle the political forces surrounding the work of the committee, but committee members should be aware of them and their effect on the committee's work. At least one of our cases included an overt example of harassment because of membership on a task force. Establishing clear ground rules about confidentiality, scheduling private meetings along with public meetings, allowing the chair or his or her designee to present ideas as collective points of consideration (rather than the ideas of specific members) are all means of accomplishing this.

- *What is the relationship between the ad hoc committee and the existing governance structure?* It should be clear what the relationship is between the committee and the existing governance structure. To whom does the committee report? If significant changes are being contemplated, the committee should communicate with members of existing governance bodies (e.g., the faculty senate, standing committees).

CONCLUSION

Legitimacy is earned. An ad hoc committee can become subject to manipulation and used to circumvent the existing governance system. Less dramatically, but just as important, missteps by the committee can make it less likely that it will render an decision that enjoys the active support of the wider community, which diminishes the prospects of enduring change.

By carefully structuring its work so that is representative, transparent, and inclusive, a committee can earn the respect and trust of the wider campus community. By soliciting ideas from a broad group of individuals, an ad hoc committee can serve a vital role in leading campus-wide deliberation about key issues. In this way, the entire campus community will be given the opportunity to weigh a new direction for the institution and contribute to the shaping of a wise decision.

NOTES

1. The authors are listed in alphabetical order. Both contributed equally to the development of this chapter.

2. For a particularly thoughtful and thorough account, see Greenberg, 1990.

3. Pseudonyms are used for all institutions.

REFERENCES

Adams, J. S. (1963). Toward an understanding of inequity. *Journal of Abnormal and Social Psychology, 67*, 422–436.

American Association of University Professors. (1995). *Policy documents and reports*. Washington, DC: Author.

Association of Governing Boards of Universities and Colleges. (1998). *AGB statement on institutional governance*. Washington, DC: Author.

Birnbaum, R. (1988). *How colleges work: The cybernetics of academic organization and leadership*. San Francisco: Jossey-Bass.

Birnbaum, R. (1992). *How academic leadership works*. San Francisco: Jossey-Bass.

Breneman, D. (1995). *Higher education: On a collision course with new realities*. (AGB Occasional Paper, No. 22.) Washington, DC: Association of Governing Boards of Universities and Colleges.

Brockner, J., Chen, Y.-R., Mannix, E. A., Leung, K., & Skarlicki, D. P. (2000). Culture and procedural fairness: When the effects of what you do depend on how you do it. *Administrative Science Quarterly, 45*, 138–159.

Corak, K. (1992, Fall). Do big decision committees work? *Planning for Higher Education, 21*, 20–24.

Duck, J. D. (1993, November-December). Managing change: The art of balancing. *Harvard Business Review*. (71)6, 109–118.

Garvin, D. A., & Roberto, M. A. (2001). What you don't know about making decisions. *Harvard Business Review, 79*(8), 108–116.

Glesne, C., & Peshkin, A. (1992). *Becoming qualitative researchers: An introduction*. New York: Longman.

Goldstein, W. (2005, January 21). For keep's sake: A chairman's files. *The Chronicle of Higher Education*, p. B5.

Greenberg, J. (1990). Organizational justice: Yesterday, today, and tomorrow. *Journal of Management, 16*, 399–432.

Hammond, J. S., Keeney, R. L., & Raiffa, H. (2001). The hidden traps in decision making. *Harvard Business Review on decision making* (pp. 143–167). Boston: Harvard Business School Press.

Hartley, M. (2003). The promise and peril of parallel governance structures. *American Behavioral Scientist, 46*(7), 923–945.

Janis, I. L. (1972). *Victims of groupthink: A psychological study of foreign-policy decisions and fiascoes*. Boston: Houghton, Mifflin.

Keller, G. (1983). *Academic strategy: The management revolution in higher education*. Baltimore: Johns Hopkins University Press.

Kotter, J. (1996). *Leading change*. Boston: Harvard Business School Press.

Lind, E. A., & Tyler, T. R. (1988). *The social psychology of procedural justice*. New York: Academic Press.

Maxwell, J. A. (1996). *Qualitative research design: An interactive approach.* Thousand Oaks, CA: Sage Publications.

Patton, M. Q. (1990). *Qualitative evaluation and research methods* (2nd ed.). Newbury Park, CA: Sage Publications.

Rubin, H. J., & Rubin, I. S. (1995). *Qualitative interviewing: The art of hearing data.* Thousand Oaks, CA: Sage Publications.

Thibaut, J., & Walker, L. (1975). *Procedural justice: A psychological analysis.* Hillsdale, NJ: Lawrence Erlbaum Associates.

Weick, K. E. (1976). Educational organizations as loosely coupled systems. *Administrative Science Quarterly, 21,* 1–19.

Weick, K. E. (1995). *Sensemaking in organizations.* Thousand Oaks, CA: Sage Publications.

CHAPTER

Beyond the Yearbook, Homecoming, and Greek Week: A New Insider-Outsider Paradigm of Student Involvement in Institutional Decision Making

Adrianna Kezar
University of Southern California

I think what we are seeing is a whole new approach to student involvement in campus decision making. Before students were mostly an outside
force, now they are part of the fabric of campus governance through
committees, new uses of technology, expanded roles for student government and the like.

—Administrator at a comprehensive research university

I was a student on this campus twenty-five years ago and it was such a different environment for involvement in campus affairs. We had to fight to
have any influence on the way faculty or administrators made decisions.
Now faculty, staff, and administrators welcome and encourage student
input into governance. Maybe it feels safer since students are less radical
today, but I really think it has to do with a different way that students
are perceived and their voice valued.

—Faculty at a liberal arts college

I think that one of the positive outcomes of management fads such as
Total Quality Management or the concept of the learning organization is
an appreciation for the voices that are closest to decision making. Institutional leaders have become more open to new voices in governance in
the last couple decades. It is often not a conscious shift, but it is occurring
and I think improving the way that we make decisions.

—Administrator at a community college

These three quotes demonstrate a shift in the thinking and beliefs of faculty
and administrators related to student involvement in campus governance. The role of students in institutional decision making has evolved

over the last several hundred years. In the 1800s, students had no formal role, and in the early to mid-1900s, they gained limited influence through student organizations and student government. Only in the last 40 years, based largely on student activism in the 1960s, has student involvement in governance been assumed to be important at the majority of campuses (surely there have always been exceptions). The 1990 *Statement on Government of Colleges and Universities* issued by the American Association of University Professors (AAUP), a key document on shared governance, reflects this change as it comments on the role of students within this process. The statement notes that "when students desire to participate responsibly in the government of the institution they attend, their desire should be recognized as a claim to opportunity both for educational experience and for involvement in the affairs in the college or university and ways should be found to permit significant student participation within the limits of attainable effectiveness" (p. 6). The *Statement* continues by saying that student involvement is critical because "if institutional support is to have its fullest possible meaning, it should incorporate the strength, freshness of view, and idealism of the student body" (p. 7). However, the AAUP *Statement* does not discuss avenues or mechanisms of involvement, but it expresses a truly new concept—the significance of student input to institutional operations and integrity.

In this chapter, I first examine the ways that student involvement in governance has been conceptualized and evolved over time—through student organizations, as activism, and via formal bodies such as student government and student trustees. The majority of literature and dialogue is typically focused on student activism and formal structures such as student government. In the second part of the chapter, I review new trends in student participation in governance through committees, ad hoc groups, advisory groups, and other emerging avenues that I label a new paradigm of governance, called *insider-outsider*. There are two reasons for highlighting this emerging trend. First, it illustrates a mostly undocumented approach or mechanism for student input that is broadening, and, in some ways, reshaping institutional decision making. Second, it appears that campuses using these new avenues are successful at teaching and modeling citizenship and participatory democracy, and thus, this approach is beneficial beyond campus governance in ways that have not been documented.

STUDENT ACTIVISM AND STUDENT GOVERNMENT

Until 30 years ago, most writings on governance would not have discussed student involvement at all (Birnbaum, 1988). However, the 1960s changed that when student activism resulting from changed social circumstances dramatically altered the student role on campus, as students demanded a right to have input into campus policy making (Mortimer & McConnell, 1979). Several structural changes occurred as a result of these demands, including the redevelopment and strengthening of student government and emergence of new structures, such as student trustees and student lobbies. These experiments were studied extensively in the early to mid-1970s (Altbach, 1997). However, student involvement in campus governance did not begin with 1960s activism. Instead, that was the beginning of formal, officially sanctioned input into campus governance on a national scale and an era of greater empowerment for students.

The earliest form (late 1800s) of influence on campus governance was student activism, usually under the auspices of organized student groups, and partially through student newspapers. Although students were not provided with the opportunity to sit on policy-making bodies, they intermittently influenced institutional decision-making processes through demonstrations, sit-ins, petitions, and other forms of protest. Student organizations provided a mechanism for bringing students together on issues of concern. Altbach (1997) noted that demonstrations or protests about the poor quality of campus food (such as the infamous Butter Rebellion at Harvard in 1766), a faculty member's ineffective teaching, or seemingly unwarranted or overburdensome course requirements were uncommon, but they occurred from time to time in a relatively unorganized fashion up until the early 1900s. After 1900, organized student groups began to form, and they provided a locus for not only campus issues, but also for broader societal concerns. Certainly, not all forms of activism were related to issues of campus governance; in fact, most generations of student activists were focused on political issues beyond the scope of the campus. At times, these political concerns also raised issues for campus policy making. For example, in the 1980s, the issue of divestment of campus monies from corporations involved in South Africa, because of the issues of apartheid, married the international and local campus concerns and policies. Altbach (1997) explains that student activism has generally "been ineffectual in the academic and political life of universities. Very rarely have student organizations taken an interest in university reform, curriculum, or governance. In some periods, notably the 1920s and 1960s, students strongly criticized the direction of higher education and the quality of instruction" (p. 4). In the 1920s and 1960s, universities were criticized for vastly increasing in size, creating a more impersonal experience, and greater reliance on the lecture method. Altbach suggests that student activism's low impact on campus decision making likely resulted because students focused on issues external to the campus, not because activism was an ineffective approach.

Beyond the informal efforts of student activism, students also influence campus decision making through student government. Formal student government has a long history dating back to the late 1890s. From the 1800s to the 1960s, student government was often the focus of local or campus political issues. These organizations were concerned with the quality of campus life and student services, and, at times, ensured representation of students in a wider forum within the university. Since the 1960s, the work of student government on many campuses had expanded. As the idea of in loco parentis was repealed (discussed further below), students took much stronger roles in determining their undergraduate experience and its direction through the work of student organizations. Additionally, student organizations became involved in decisions from which they historically had been excluded, such as academic, financial, and technological issues, the protection of students' rights, and student judicial proceedings. In the last 20 years, student government became more complex and formal through student senates, service on executive advisory groups, student courts, and appointments within the faculty senate, academic unit, or school/college committees, and administrative committees.

The Reign of in Loco Parentis

Yet, one wonders why student voice was always on the periphery rather than included in institutional operations. A major barrier to formal student involvement in campus decision making was the philosophy of *in loco parentis* that set the tone for the role of students on college campuses from the beginning in the 1600s through the 1960s. This philosophy viewed students as children in the care of adults—faculty and administrators. Thus, students needed to be given strict and comprehensive boundaries and rules that encompassed a tremendous range of behaviors, including, but not limited to, study and sleeping hours, dating, and even how close together students could dance. Students were considered unfit to create campus policy. Little student input was gathered or considered relevant. Student empowerment movements in the 1960s effectively dismantled the philosophy of in loco parentis and students came to be considered adults, and views about their involvement in campus decision making changed. Although boundaries and rules still exist, such as policies on plagiarism, the nature of policy making has changed to focus on academics rather than on personal behavior, and students are part of creating policies that govern them.

As the philosophy of in loco parentis faded because of student demands in the 1960s, institutions reconsidered the role of students, and membership on campus committees and as part of campus decision-making processes, such as search committees, became commonplace on many campuses. For example, in the late 1960s, most campuses examined student participation in the government of the institution and developed formal policies allowing for more input from students. For instance, at the University of Wisconsin, the administration withdrew all in loco parentis activities and policies of the campus; added students to all campus committees; gave student government greater autonomy; and restructured student disciplinary procedures and limited their scope, giving students more direct control over their own judicial processes (University of Wisconsin, 1968). On campuses across the country, students were added to academic policy and curriculum committees, such as admissions, outreach, housing, faculty-student relations, scholarship, and financial aid groups. By 1972, 14 percent of all institutions in the country had a student member on the board of trustees, with public institutions having a higher percentage of about 25 percent (Blandford, 1972). Students had voting privileges only on some boards, but usually not on all issues. Over the last 30 years, the number of students serving on boards has continued to increase across the country. The 1970s represented an important time, during which various new structures were experimented with in order to include students' voices.

Even though broad changes regarding student involvement occurred, most research and writing focuses on the concrete changes, such as student trustees, student lobbying, and the revised role of student government, in which students were asked to send representatives to campus policy-making bodies, such as the senate (Carpenter, 1972; Mossman, 1980; University of Wisconsin, 1968; Stephen, et al., 1969).

Forces Reshaping Student Involvement

As the quotations at the beginning of this chapter suggest, change is afoot. Several factors have coalesced and continue to do so to make students' voices an even more central part of campus governance in the 1980s, the 1990s, and into the 21st century, extending the many changes that had occurred in the late 1960s and throughout the 1970s. First, new forms of technology, such as the Internet and e-mail, allow for greater communication and ease of input. Thus, many decision-making processes have opened up in recent years. In addition, management approaches in the past two decades have emphasized the importance of breaking down hierarchical structures and seeking a wide range of input. For example, total quality management (TQM) encourages managers and leaders to provide decision-making power to people throughout the organization, in particular, those closest to the specific decision being made. TQM has led to greater participation of people in governance processes and in democratizing many organizations. Third, the gulf between students and "the establishment" of faculty and administration is now smaller on most campuses, providing more common ground for governance decisions (Levine & Cureton, 1998). All of these elements reflect broader trends in society that are also appearing on college campuses. Some campuses have had long traditions of student involvement and have always been less hierarchical and parental, providing more inclusive environments. But, even on these campuses, new forms of involvement, such as those spurred by new uses of technology, have emerged.

A New Paradigm: Insider-Outsider

Accompanying these trends is an emerging new paradigm of involving students in institutional decision making. A widely accepted philosophy for student involvement in governance has not followed the dismantling of in loco parentis. For a short period of time immediately following in loco parentis, a student empowerment philosophy held sway, marked by the proposition that students were adults and should be included in the major decision-making groups that made policy specific to students. Student empowerment declined in the late 1970s, and no consistent philosophy of student involvement has since emerged and been articulated. Yet, one is emerging currently, and this chapter gives voice to that new paradigm. I have labeled the new paradigm the *insider-outsider perspective*.

As noted previously, for many years, students were simply excluded from institutional decision making, and the only possibility for them to influence campus governance was through student activism or through a parallel system of student government that could create policies focused specifically on students and thus was limited (i.e., homecoming, the yearbook, and Greek Week). This formal system effectively worked to keep them *outside* the important governance system of the institution. Student activists in the 1960s helped create a meaningful role for students in the formal governance processes of the institution through the presence of student trustees and membership on key committees. The student voice moved from outside important decision-making structures to inside them. Student decision makers became *insiders*. However, some leaders argued that the role of student trustee, for example, was token, especially since many student regents or trustees cannot vote. An alternative belief was that by including students in official governance roles administrators were co-opting students into the establishment and thus effectively diffusing their activist role and pacifying their voice. Many advocates and supporters of students' activism have worried in recent years that the valuable role of student as agitator was being lost.

The new paradigm for students that has emerged in recent years combines the *insider and outsider roles* and *deepens and increases involvement* in governance. Students, as members of university committees and possessing campus leadership roles, are acting both as insiders in having a voice in decision making through various committee appointments, and as outsiders because they find power in numbers and thus can create strong dissenting opinions and work outside the system to change it. The current anti-sweatshop movement is an example. Student leaders are not isolated (and potentially co-opted) through a narrow role like student regent. This new combination is powerful in that it brings the best students have to offer in terms of seeing the campus with fresh and different eyes, but also being able to impact the formal decision-making processes and work outside them. Successful campus leaders recognize that, as students take on this more significant and deeper role in governance, they need education, mentoring, and support to be effective. Otherwise, there can be risks if students are brought into a decision-making process without the appropriate background.

In the last 30 years, most attention (in the news and in the literature) has focused on the role of student government or students' serving as board members; yet, students' roles in governance have grown in many different ways that are mostly undocumented. These newer trends of involvement tend to be more broad-based and reflect this new philosophy of thinking about student involvement in governance—the combined insider-outsider perspective. I will describe these emerging trends as a new paradigm for student involvement in governance.

THE NEW PARADIGM OF STUDENT INVOLVEMENT IN GOVERNANCE: INSIDER-OUTSIDER PERSPECTIVE

Over time, campuses have developed a host of practices for involving students more broadly in institutional decision making. It has become common for campuses to appoint student representatives to campus-wide committees and ad hoc groups, even when the governance process does not require it (Ouclat, Faris, & McMahon, 2001). Student affairs divisions have been particularly active in ensuring that students are represented on policy-making groups that involve students' interests. In this section, I review some characteristics and best practices of this new paradigm of student involvement in governance.

There is no single approach for involving more students in governance, but some promising practices can be identified. Some campuses have created open electronic forums and blogs for obtaining input from students on campus policies. At certain campuses, the forums are moderated and used to create a learning-oriented dialogue. On others, the technology is used more as a tool for allowing feedback and expression of views. E-mail is a key tool for creating greater involvement. In addition to electronic forums, some campuses have bulletin boards (electronic and otherwise) and have adopted other forms of communication to collect feedback and post views. Although less interactive than dialogues, this approach allows students to get involved in expressing and articulating views on an issue. Students are allowed a high degree of freedom to play the combined insider-outsider role with e-mail; because people are not face-to-face, they are often not intimidated to provide feedback to faculty and administrators that might not otherwise emerge in person where power dynamics are more powerful. E-mail and blogs represents one of the most promising approaches, as they can be more inclusive than most other mechanisms. Yet, they have downsides. E-mail can serve as a mechanism by which people feel free to make uninformed comments because they are anonymous and distant, not taking the requisite time to become knowledgeable about issues or have to be responsible for their opinions. Also, electronic postings can be a superficial exchange because the human interaction and feedback is delayed or even absent. Other approaches can require that students commit certain amounts of time or effort. To participate responsibly in governance, individuals need to understand the nuances of issues—be informed and be committed to following the decisions to the end.

Advisory groups (student and campus-wide) represent another vehicle for broader student involvement and also illustrate the new philosophy of involvement. Many campuses have sanctioned advisory groups that are part of the formal governance process. For example, presidents establish student advisory groups (usually made up of 10–20 students) that provide input on key issues facing the campus. Another approach is that a student(s) sit on an already existing advisory group or council.

In addition to these formal bodies, informal advisory groups are also being established at many campuses. Many schools, colleges, departments, and programs are asking students to serve on ad hoc advisory groups that inform decision makers or decision-making bodies. On campuses where students may not be designated or included in formal campus policy-making bodies, staff and faculty are intentionally seeking their input in decision making. The advisory process usually involves tapping a set of students to meet with the leader or decision-making body and to provide input on issues that they are considering, such as changes in grading policy, schedule of classes, curriculum content, or technology or lab hours for a campus. Campus leaders and decision-making bodies are realizing that they are able to create better policy by obtaining student input up-front, thus smoothing the implementation of the new policies and decreasing resistance. Ad hoc student advisory groups most often are asked to comment on policies that affect students directly, but, at times, they are invited to comment on other types of policies, such as campus technology plans or auxiliary services. Because groups of students rather than individual students are asked to comment, they are positioned as both insiders and outsiders and thus feel more empowered to challenge administrative/ faculty power and prerogative. Advisory groups are growing on many campuses as leaders realize the importance of stakeholder input into decision making.

Another promising approach for increasing student involvement and allowing them to play the insider-outsider role is through serving on faculty senate committees, the cabinet, and college- and school-wide committees. Many campuses are changing their governance guidelines so that students are included as members of various decision-making groups, ranging from search committees, to campus-wide retention or assessment committees, and to school-specific committees such as technology, curriculum, or academic affairs. However, some decision-making bodies, for example, the faculty senate on many campuses, do not designate student involvement. But growing numbers of institutions are providing students the opportunity to serve on committees informally. In addition to formal governance committees, students are being asked to serve on ad hoc committees related to enrollment management, curricular reform, and diversity. Such committees provide the most avenues for involving students and can reach hundreds of students.

Another mechanism, although more uncommon, is to involve students in campus retreats and town meetings where major issues related to direction and mission are discussed. Many campuses have found students invaluable in asking tough questions about how a new vision fundamentally assists in creating a better learning environment, and the students often help to ground discussions in the mission of teaching and learning.

Campuses vary in the ways they institutionalize student involvement in decision making. For example, some integrate the notion of student governance into the formal curriculum/ cocurriculum and provide credit for serving on campus committees and develop assignments to accompany service. Others treat involvement as an extracurricular activity that builds leadership and citizenship, but do not offer credit or have assignments designated. Some campuses have a formalized approach to foster student involvement in institutional decision making with a strategic plan for ways to increase or deepen involvement. Some institutions have policies that require students to serve on decision-making bodies, making it part of the fabric and culture of the campus. Others chose a more informal approach that allows for participation to change over time. Some campuses have a combined approach, in which some formal policies exist related to student involvement in governance and many other informal practices emerge over time; this seems to be the most prevalent approach.

Benefits of Student Involvement

The remainder of this chapter provides illustrations of the new forms of student governance drawn from a recent study of student engagement. Before describing examples of this emerging paradigm, it is important to explore why campuses might want to engage in this type of activity. One reason that has already been mentioned throughout this chapter is the desire to improve institutional decision making by involving those affected by the proposed policies. For many institutions, this provides ample justification.

Another reason that emerged from this study was the belief that including students in governance is an important strategy to fulfill the institution's mission to develop engaged citizens and future leaders. Institutional decision makers argue that there is no better way to encourage this outcome among students than to have them involved in campus governance processes. Even though all students will not be involved in campus governance, democratic and leadership principles are modeled for other students across campus. Most campuses across the country note citizen and leadership development as part of their mission statement, but have few ways of fostering this goal beyond traditional student organizations or community service activities. Including students in real institutional decision making can help campuses meet this stated goal. Additionally, campus leaders have expressed concerns about political apathy, lack of engagement, poor citizenship skills, and limited leadership development among students; finding ways to combat these attributes has helped to foster a growing interest among institutional leaders for involving students in governance.

It should also be noted that mission-focused institutions such as women's colleges, historically black colleges and universities, and Hispanic-serving institutions tend to involve students in governance to a significant degree. It may be that these populations have been excluded from citizenship and leadership roles, and these institutions make it a priority to prepare the individuals within their institutions for this role. In addition, these types of campuses value inclusion, participation, and consensus, of which involvement of students in governance is an extension. Although all types of institutions are involving students in new ways, institutions that serve historically underrepresented populations can serve as important role models for other types of institutions interested in more actively involving students and fulfilling their mission to develop leadership and citizenship skills.

THE NEW PARADIGM OF STUDENT INVOLVEMENT IN ACTION: SIX CASES

Some specific examples and brief cases help illustrate the new student involvement paradigm in practice. I included a variety of cases from a research study, as the examples demonstrate both campus structure and philosophy to support the new paradigm. Some examples are included because student involvement is very broad, while others were chosen because the mechanisms or structures used on the campuses were distinctive, and still others because the philosophy supporting involvement was helpful and can serve as a model for other campuses. These cases are drawn from a national study on student engagement called documenting effective educational practices (DEEP), which examined a host of institutions across the country in order to understand the institutions' higher than predicted scores on the national survey of student engagement. The project was conducted by the DEEP research team in conjunction with Indiana University and the American Association for Higher Education, with support from the Lumina Foundation. I have changed the names of the institutions to protect their anonymity.

Egalitarian College

At Egalitarian College, a former women's college, student involvement in governance is omnipresent. This college demonstrates how a campus can make students part of the very fabric of campus governance. Students have always had a degree of involvement, but in the last 20 years, it has moved to a broader and deeper level. The ethos of the campus is egalitarian; when one walks on the campus, she or he realizes that faculty, staff, and students all view themselves and each other as learners and participants in the collegiate experience. This egalitarian ethos was characteristic of many campuses that involved students broadly in campus governance.

Students are involved in almost every campus standing committee except for a few, where they would be perceived to be inappropriate, such as the American Association of University Professors (AAUP) chapter, the union group representing faculty. The educational policy committee and budget advisory committee—often the groups or committees at other campuses where students would be excluded—include student members, who have an equal voice in discussions. In addition to standing committees, students serve on campus-wide, ad hoc committees, such as curricular revision committees. Their involvement is not an afterthought; student participation is written into the charge for each ad hoc committee. Students serve on every search committee for both faculty and administrative positions. Students are elected to serve on these various committees by other students, not handpicked by the administration. The campus relies upon elections to model good behavior that they hope students will replicate in life as responsible citizens. Finally, a student trustee sits on the board.

Because students are so involved in the campus decision making, no separate student governance body exists. Rather than a parallel system of student government, there is just one governance mechanism.

Faculty and staff discussed how the system worked to the benefit of all groups of stakeholders. One faculty member noted: "Students can go to the administration with a proposed change and get support to work on an initiative, and the administration approaches the students and says it wants help from them on an initiative they want to pass." As an illustrative example, one student said:

> We wanted to create a smoke-free campus initiative and we simply went to the administration and they gave us support to start working it through the campus governance process. We just work well together and support each other. Yet, this does not mean that we cannot challenge the administration out of their comfort zone. When there is an equal sense of power, you can challenge respectfully.

These two comments demonstrate the important symbiotic relationship of various stakeholders in a policy process and the ability of students to play both the insider-outsider role in challenging the governance process as well as being a part of the formal system.

This example demonstrates the power of an institutional philosophy and organizational culture supporting student involvement, the creation of various mechanisms to broaden and deepen involvement, and how the voices of students work within, but also challenge the governance process.

Leadership University

A different example of the new governance paradigm is from Leadership University, an Hispanic-serving institution. The university is committed to leadership development, particularly, that of historically underrepresented groups. The ethos and philosophy of the campus is one of racial uplift and the need for students who may feel disenfranchised to develop their voice as citizen-leaders. Faculty, staff, and students commented on ways that expectations for student involvement helped foster extensive involvement. One student stated: "I have heard about other campuses where there are only a few opportunities for involvement and staff cannot get students involved in governance. Here, a lot of students are involved; it is just part of the student experience and our learning."

Based on this institution's commitment to student involvement in institutional decision making, the administration has established several mechanisms for increasing student participation. For example, on all campus committees, 20 percent of all representatives are students. To ensure that the student voice is not marginalized, this campus guarantees that students constitute a significant portion of each committee, rather than designate a single student to each committee. Students talked about how this made a difference to their experience. One noted:

> I have spoken to friends on other campuses and they might be one of 20 or 25 people on a committee. They say they feel intimidated and never say anything. Therefore, the involvement is really token. Here I am one of several voices. I always feel free to speak up. This approach also ensures that many different students are provided with the opportunity to serve in a leadership capacity.

An administrator noted how this significant role for students was part of the formal curriculum: "We see this involvement as part of the students' learning to be good citizens and to help ensure that they can make changes in society. This is the type of learning that can help them as well as our world. Governance is learned through living it." Students on campus were also included in campus retreats and advisory groups. One faculty member commented:

> Although committee service is the formal way we ensure students are involved in governance, they are also included in ad hoc activities that the campus creates such as conferences, retreats, ad hoc groups, and the like. It is part of our philosophy to involve students in governance, so it emerges within each structure.

As this faculty member notes, a belief about the importance of student involvement in governance is critical to ensuring they are included in campus policy development. Additionally, student involvement in various governance structures provides an important and visible symbol for the values of the campus. As with the previous case, this example demonstrates how both philosophy and structures are critical for ensuring student involvement in academic decision making.

Destiny College

At Destiny College, a women's college, there is a history of student involvement that has increased in recent years. This campus demonstrates the power of an institutional philosophy to ensure student voice and involvement in governance. The ethos of the campus is that women can create their own destinies and are responsible for making the changes they want to see in the world. Over time this belief has translated into action and involvement in student governance. In 1906, students petitioned for legislative and executive control over nonacademic matters and were granted responsibility for making decisions. This involvement helped create an ethic of empowerment and a dedication among faculty to help students create their own destinies. This philosophy remains today. One student commented: "All campus discussions are open for debate among all members of the community." Until recently, student involvement was limited and they were excluded from academic matters. However, in more recent years, they are involved with these decisions as well.

The institution's initial philosophy has evolved and now reflects the principles of the new paradigm of student involvement. Students are involved with all campus-wide committees, ad hoc groups, and included in the cabinet. The president and other campus leaders seek student input on all issues that go before the board. A regular informal occurrence for student-administrator engagement is "Pizza with the President," in which the president asks students for feedback about the quality of their experiences and ideas for improvement.

Global University

Global University, a comprehensive research university, also exemplifies the new paradigm in student governance. One of the main goals of the campus is to prepare students for global leadership and citizenship. The campus is committed to creating multicultural and international events and learning opportunities. The notion of a global village reflects the strong campus belief of respect for people from all cultures and walks of life, regardless of position or place in the institutions. Many faculty and staff commented on how the culture of global citizenship and egalitarianism supported student involvement in governance. Said one person: "We are a campus of many different kinds of people, representing different countries and backgrounds. Deeply respecting these differences makes one appreciate the need for different voices in governance."

Many decision-making structures reflect this philosophy. For example, every school and college has its own student advisory committee. Students noted the importance of these committees to their education and interest in citizenship/leadership. One said:

> The dean has made all twelve of us critical advisors for her decision making. We meet monthly and she reviews new policies, directions, and ideas. We bring ideas to her for change. The conversation has made me learn a great deal over the last two years, often more than in the classroom.

The president has an advisory board of 20 students, which reflects the important role students play in shaping institutional policy at the senior-most level. Many administrators, faculty, and students noted both the symbolic importance of this group for student involvement across campus as well as the feeling that student voices are valued on campus. The president described how the group worked:

> I felt that developing a more formal way to obtain input from the students would create better decisions, provide learning opportunities, and help others around campus to see the importance of student voice. Apparently it has worked as most deans and department chairs also have advisory groups now.

Students are also actively involved on campus committees, where each one has a student representative. Some are appointed while others are elected. Student government acts as a link for electing students to serve on certain committees. The student government is quite active and plays a significant role in creating student-oriented polices and programs. Students independently manage several campus governance processes, such as the student judicial board and student activities. Students commented on the importance of a strong student government. One said:

> We are excited to be involved broadly in governance, but sometimes you
> need to be able to question the administration and policies. We can often
> better do this within the student government. So, I think it works best to
> have two strong systems—students involved in campus governance and a
> student government.

As a result, students achieve the insider and outsider status in ways different from
other institutions that had only one system of governance. This university had
a very comprehensive approach to involving students in governance with advisory boards, committee service, and an active student government, which was all
shaped by a philosophy of egalitarianism.

Grass Roots College

At Grass Roots, an historically black institution, student governance has taken
new shape in recent years. Grass Roots College is committed to racial uplift and
voice for African American students in the democratic process. Like many similar
colleges, Grass Roots had a strong history of in loco parentis that led administrators and faculty to exclude students in most decision-making processes. Over the
last few decades, however, the college has reexamined its commitment to African American leadership and recognized the need to empower students to make
responsible choices and to learn about how policies are made and change created.
As a strategy to fulfill this philosophy, the college began to intentionally expand
the venues available to students in the governance process.

Like Global University, each individual college at Grass Roots established an
advisory board. For example, the College of Arts and Sciences developed a student
advisory committee where the students, not the administrators or faculty as is typical elsewhere, set the agenda and lead the discussions. This approach is uncommon, even at a campus with strong egalitarian traditions like those described
previously. Administrators seek advice through this bottom-up, or grass roots,
governance process rather than the typical top-down model. Another interesting approach is that their campus peer advisors take a leadership role and are
intentionally tapped and called upon to give council to governing bodies. The
peer advisors are hired to work with students on campus and then are recruited
to work in the governance process. They are intentionally mentored to take on
this more prominent role on campus. The peer advisors serve on some faculty
and administrative committees and governance groups and for other governance
groups, they may be asked to attend particular meetings and for advice on policy
development.

The campus also used technology innovatively to expand participation. Students are sent e-mail messages seeking their input on important policy changes.
Students described how they are informed of all campus initiatives and feel free
to make comments and question proposed policy directions. This approach was
successful not just because it provided students ongoing opportunities for input,
but because students said they saw changes in policies, programs, and practices

based on their input. The use of technology has helped to further create expectations that students will have input into governance. As one student noted: "It has developed a sense of responsibility in me for the issues of the larger [campus] community that I will translate into other communities I affiliate with in the future."

There was also a sense that students could and should push the envelope, and challenge campus policies because their input had become such an important and routine part of campus operations. A student commented on this belief:

> It is hard for me to imagine not being able to have an equal voice in campus governance. Alumni come to campus shocked at the kinds of initiatives students have started on campus and our ability to change campus policies. It seems just part of the way things are here, but I realize we are lucky to have this broad involvement where we can really make change.

Change Agent University

At Change Agent University, a comprehensive university, the institution is firmly embedded in the belief that students need to be prepared to play a role in leadership internationally and locally. Students are educated to be change agents, making the world a better place. One student reflected on the impact of this philosophy both on him and on the campus: "Faculty tell us we are change agents and need to begin that work here on campus. I talk to students at other campuses and they just do not have the kind of empowerment we have here. I know it makes me look at the world differently. I wouldn't trade this experience for anything."

As a result of this philosophy and commitment, students are involved in committees, advisory boards, and most campus policy-making bodies. Perhaps the most interesting mechanism they have developed is a Web site for gaining student input into governance. Students participate in an open forum on the campus Web site where various campus issues are discussed from items going before the board to more specific program or department policies and practices. Students are informed by faculty members in class that the open forum is their chance to influence their community and provided assignments connecting an issue being discussed or debates on the forum to the class. The Web site, with its dialogue, has become part of the fabric of the curriculum, with faculty making related course material. The dining halls are filled with discussion about governance issues at each meal, but especially at night, where frequent debates can be heard.

CONCLUSION: ACHIEVING THE NEW INSIDER-OUTSIDER PARADIGM

All of these institutions created the insider-outsider paradigm for student involvement on their campuses through different approaches, based upon their unique histories and cultures. Although the approach to involvement is unique, they share some common elements that can be instructive for other campuses trying to create this paradigm. First, each tends to have a strong belief (institutional philosophy) that supports widespread student involvement. In some instances, this philosophy has a long history on campus, but at others, it recently emerged, in which case it may represent a distinctive change in thinking about student involvement in institutional decision making. As the examples demonstrate, these philosophies usually reflect such concepts as egalitarianism, citizenship development, leadership or change agents, student-centeredness, and learning. Second, institutions have a similar purpose in involving students in governance—to create critical learning opportunities for students, especially those related to citizenship and leadership development. Third, these institutions also tended to use a similar repertoire of mechanisms for increasing involvement—committees, ad hoc groups, advisory committees, Web forums or dialogues, and retreats/town meetings.

These examples might lead other campuses to reconsider their approach to governance. Yes, it takes more work on the part of administrators and faculty, and they as the traditional powerbrokers "give away" some of their influence, but strong student involvement has tremendous opportunities to positively impact the campus. As noted at the beginning of this chapter, many institutions are already moving in this direction. Some have tried out a particular strategy such as advisory boards or committees, and it is the intention of this chapter that the ideas presented in it provide strategies that will result in more opportunities for students to learn about governance and democracy through practicing academic governance.

At many campuses, student involvement still involves a small (even token) number of students—the new paradigm is not yet widespread. For those campuses still questioning the value of broadening governance to include students, this chapter has illustrated that student involvement is an important strategy for campuses to embody their goals of instilling citizenship and leadership. According to faculty and administrators from the above campuses, involving students in decision making leads to better decisions. Armed with rationale, strategy, and new mechanisms for involvement, campuses should feel comfortable adopting this new paradigm of student involvement.

Yet, many of these institutions described in this chapter are unique, and the students that attend them may be more politically active, interested in leadership, community-oriented, and engaged than students attending other institutions. Given the uniqueness of these institutions and their student bodies, will the new paradigm be able to spread to other types of institutions? Does the current political and social climate support such a model of student governance? Students at many of these institutions attend school full-time and do not have significant work commitments (although this was not the case at all institutions). It is unclear whether and how the increase in the number of hours that students work will impact this new paradigm of student involvement in governance. Also many urban institutions and comprehensive institutions are increasingly attended by older and nontraditional students who are likely to have less time for involvement. Will this mean that the new paradigm of student involvement in governance might be limited to certain types of institutions and environments? Perhaps, but technology might be able to help older and nontraditional students be involved with campus governance because it allows them to be involved based on their schedules. For example, global and change agent universities both have large numbers of older and nontraditional students and were able to include these groups in the governance process through the use of technology.

Over the last 30 years, students have shifted in their career orientation and vocational goals; today, students report a greater interest in volunteering and getting involved in community activism. However, this commitment may shift, and it could impact the degree to which students are involved in campus governance, which occurred in the 1980s when fewer students were interested in being involved in campus governance. It must be acknowledged that some of the forces (e.g., changing demographics, shifting focus of student values) that are affecting higher education may slow the impact of this new paradigm of student involvement in governance or may alter this paradigm in the future.

REFERENCES

Altbach, P. (1997). *Student politics in America*. New Brunswick, NJ: McGraw-Hill.

American Association of University Professors. (1990). *Statement on government of colleges and universities*. Washington, DC: Author.

Birnbaum, R. (1988). *How colleges work: The cybernetics of academic organization and leadership*. San Francisco: Jossey-Bass.

Blandford, B. (1972). *Student participation on institutional governing boards* (Survey Number 11). Washington, DC: American Council on Education. (ERIC Document Reproduction Service No. ED0 70410)

Carpenter, G. (1972). *College student government as a leisure sport*. (ERIC Document Reproduction Service No. ED062915)

Katz, J. (1967). The student activists—rights, needs and powers of undergraduates. *New Dimension in Higher Education, Report* No. 30.

Levine, A., & Cureton, J. (1998). *When hopes and fear collide*. San Francisco: Jossey-Bass.

Millett, J. (1978). *New structures of campus power: Success and failure of emerging forms of institutional governance*. San Francisco: Jossey-Bass.

Mortimer, K., & McConnell, T. (1979). *Sharing authority effectively*. San Francisco: Jossey-Bass.

Mossman, B. (1980). The value of young trustees. *AGB reports, 22*(3), 35–37.

Ouclat, C., Faris, S., & McMahon, K. (Eds.). (2001). *Developing non-hierarchical leadership on campus: Case studies and best practices in higher education*. Westport, CT: Greenwood Press.

Stephen, T. et al. (1969). *The student role in faculty selection, evaluation, and retention*. Durham: University of New Hampshire.

University of Wisconsin. (1968). *Ad hoc committee on the role of students in the government of the university*. Author. (ERIC Document Reproduction Service No. ED035383)

CHAPTER

Technology and Its Impact on Campus Decision Making: Asking New Questions and Raising More Complications

Dennis J. Gayle
The University of the West Indies

Information and communication technologies are increasingly driving the world economy. Within institutions of higher learning, educational and communication technologies (ECTs) increasingly influence university governance, management, research, teaching, and learning. Such technologies enhance administrative processes, as with the use of centralized database systems for enrollment, financial, and space management. Examples include Oracle, PeopleSoft, Banner, and SAP. Meanwhile, ECTs such as WebCT, Lotus Notes, and Blackboard also expand the scope of distance and distributed education, and enrich the educational experience of both traditional and nontraditional students. These evolving educational and communications technologies are altering many decision arenas, processes, and schedules. Issues such as intellectual property rights, academic entrepreneurialism, and campus internationalization must now be addressed with the dynamic potentials and challenges of such technologies in mind. These technologies continue to impact institutions of higher education, in both expected and unexpected ways, as software cost, quality, and accessibility vary over time.

INTRODUCTION

The twenty-first-century environment is increasingly driven by information and communications technologies (ICTs). They are the key component in the production and delivery of more and more goods and services in the modern world economy. For example, during 1985–2000, high-technology manufactured exports increased their share in world imports from 12 to 23 percent, while the equivalent share of similar medium- and low-technology exports expanded from 40 to 45 percent only (United Nations Economic Commission for Latin

America and the Caribbean, 2002). Telecommunications constitute the basic infrastructure, but ICT applications are vast and growing. Our campuses are not immune to these trends. Wireless networks as well as e-journals and e-books proliferate. E-mail is ubiquitous and accepted as essential. When computer systems are down, database-related work comes to a halt. National and international grids expand. More and more institutions articulate e-commerce strategies. Among campus community members, 24/7 access to computing is a given, together with the need for continuously upgraded firewalls and other antivirus security measures. University crises are publicized and accelerated by blogs. To what extent, and how, can governance structures facilitate the effective incorporation of educational technology into institutional programs and their delivery systems and processes, while ensuring that student, financial aid, human resources, and business databases communicate smoothly, linking *structural* and *conversational* data, such as multimedia?

Educational and communication technologies (ECTs) generate some of the most critical decision-making challenges for campus leaders, within issue-areas such as institutional management and shared governance, including the rights and responsibilities of participants; curriculum delivery; the ownership of intellectual property such as course content, teaching, and learning incentives; technology cost control; online program accreditation; the nature and expectations of university libraries and librarians; and even the idea as well as the locus of the *university*. This chapter will explore the major decision-making challenges for campus leaders that are driven or mediated by educational and communications technologies.

THE IMPACT OF ECTS ON UNIVERSITY MANAGEMENT

By fall 2002, approximately one-tenth of all universities and colleges with annual operating budgets in excess of $100 million had implemented, or were seeking to implement, comprehensive and relatively expensive interactive software systems, such as Oracle, PeopleSoft, SAP, or Banner. Such enterprise applications facilitate financial, human resources, customer, supplier, and space management, constituting a market valued at more than $75 billion per annum. The goal of higher education institutions engaged in implementing these systems was to achieve significant economies of scale and scope, as well as real-time responses to "what if" budgetary questions, whether at the academic unit, or division, or institutional level. The potential for enhanced management and governance continued to attract the attention of senior executives, at institutions ranging from the University of Michigan, Case Western Reserve University, the University of Massachusetts, and Princeton University (PeopleSoft) to the University of South Dakota, Central Michigan University, California State University at Chico, and the University of Mississippi (SAP).

However, these capacities have the potential to be expensive, further straining already stressed institutional budgets and creating highly ambiguous situations for university decision makers. Implementation costs are daunting for many institutions, averaging $15 million for a typical three-year PeopleSoft plan in 2001. In many cases, the installation process required a complete redesign of budgetary systems, from payroll and financial aid to maintenance, accompanied by extensive staff-training programs, not to mention hardware upgrades. Within several universities engaged in implementing such systems, glitches had to be addressed repeatedly, even after extended installation periods.

In 2003, Oracle's $7.7 billion hostile bid for PeopleSoft, seeking to unite the world's second- and third-largest enterprise applications makers sparked fears that a wave of consolidation could follow, creating uncertainty among their higher education subscribers and presaging increased prices for services. The PeopleSoft Higher Education User Group, representing some 345 universities and colleges, expressed concern that Oracle would force conversion to its own databases in order to earn more revenue from updates and support. In the end, Oracle purchased PeopleSoft, after 18 months of litigation, for $10.3 billion, while also accepting PeopleSoft's prior guarantee to its customers of a refund worth several times their original license fees, should support become unavailable.

Universities and colleges have also experimented with other management-related software programs such as "Capture," which streamlines the admissions process by placing application forms, transcripts, personal essays, and recommendations online. At the same time, database security has become an increasingly important issue, with universities including Stanford, Chicago, and Harvard reporting either invasion by hackers, including applicants seeking early admission information, or incidences of accidental, unauthorized access to confidential student and staff information, leading to potential loss of privacy, if not identity theft, during the 2004–2005 academic year. Increasing interest in alternatives to Internet Explorer, such as Firefox, an open-source program released in 2004, has resulted, given continuing security problems.

However, ECTs also have the potential to be harmful. For instance, distance education technologies have facilitated the creation of "diploma mills," unaccredited providers posing as legitimate colleges and universities. This was the concern that led the Louisiana Board of Regents to refuse renewal of the operating licenses of Bienville, Columbus, Glenford, and Lacrosse Universities, on October 1, 2002 (Foster, 2002).

One "dashboard" indicator as to just how important ECTs have become to university and college decision making is the number of related journal articles appearing. For instance, a series of articles appeared in *Trusteeship*, published by the Association of Governing Boards of Universities and Colleges (AGB) in November/December 2000; in *Change, the Magazine of Higher Education,* published in September/October 2000 by the Association of Higher Education; and in *Academe, the Bulletin of the American Association of University Professors* in May/June 2001. The headline on the cover of the *Academe* issue is illustrative: "In IT Together—Faculty, Administrators, and Shared Governance." Meanwhile the cover of *Change* proclaimed: "E-Learning—The Tradeoff between Richness and Reach."

However, college and university ECT budgets have been contracting, putting the pinch on an already costly set of necessary investments. Market Data Retrieval's annual survey of officials at 1,427 accredited community colleges and baccalaureate institutions indicated that information technology spending by all U.S. higher education institutions was approximately $5.15 billion in the 2004–2005 academic year, compared with $5.36 billion in the 2003–2004 academic year, a decline of 4 percent, and the second consecutive annual reduction in such expenditure. Similarly, the annual Campus Computing Survey found that 24 percent of all colleges and universities reduced their academic computing budgets in 2004, compared with downturn undertaken by 41 percent in 2003 and 33 percent in 2002. Market Data Retrieval also estimated that during 2004–2005, higher education institutions would spend $2.4 billion on hardware, $1.3 billion on software, $1.2 billion on external services, such as service contracts, and $242 million on technology training. Institutions with enrollments of more than 25,000 reported an average ECT budget of $6.1 million, while universities and colleges with enrollments of less than 25,000 reported an average ECT budget of $456,000. Where private institutions expended $553 per student on educational and communications technology, public institutions spent $203 per student, almost two-thirds less. Even so, 79 percent of the 5,400 colleges and universities surveyed by Market Data Retrieval in October 2004 reported having wireless networks, increasing from 70 percent in 2003 and 45 percent in 2002 (Kiernan, 2005).

In an effort to further elucidate evolving attitudes at universities and colleges concerning the impact of ECTs upon university management and decision making, I sent a questionnaire during the summer of 2004 to chief information officers and associate vice presidents for academic affairs and finance, respectively (or their counterparts) at 100 research, master's level, liberal arts, and baccalaureate institutions.[1] A response rate of 27 percent resulted, and frequency distributions generated. The majority of respondents were considering the installation of SAP, PeopleSoft, or Oracle, and were very concerned to establish whether such enterprise-applications software (ERPs) would be cost-effective, and significantly improve internal business processes, such as financial aid, space, enrollment, payroll and human resources management, or would run over budget, consume more administrative time in training than anticipated, and cause business processes to be adjusted to fit the software, whether or not this was inherently desirable. Among the institutions that had already installed such ERPs (12 of the original 100), most were using SAP, and justified this decision mainly in terms of support service quality and projected productivity increases, while agreeing that the ready availability of real-time information could enhance the university governance process. However, none of the responding institutions had yet completed the cost-recovery period. Only two had articulated performance measures in a widely circulated strategic plan.

The survey results also indicated that the majority of decisions to purchase educational software were driven by faculty champions, and its adoption sustained by one or more colleges or schools. In turn, appropriate support personnel were often recruited or identified only after a critical mass of software users had accumulated. Almost half the responding institutions made use of two or more competing software packages. Few had yet established performance measures of any kind, although faculty senates and a variety of task forces were considering adopting such measures. In a majority of cases, a steadily increasing number and range of courses had been made available online, mostly for the purpose of providing distributed education to nontraditional students. However, at 10 percent of the responding institutions, many faculty members were reportedly making use of bulletin boards and discussion groups to engage their students in helping each other to learn, and in extended teamwork. Continuing concerns of the respondents included the availability of qualified educational technology staff, faculty training needs, and the sufficiency of funding, by means such as student technology fees.

THE IMPACT OF ECTS ON ACADEMIC ACTIVITIES

How have such technologies affected academic activities? College libraries have been creating online archives to catalog, preserve, and share their film and video collections that walk a fine line between fair use and copyright issues. Librarians promote digitization as a means of saving space, containing purchase costs, and protecting the environment. When Google Print announced a decade-long project to digitize millions of books in a searchable database, the Association of American University Presses, which represents 125 nonprofit academic publishers, expressed concerns that the projected scanning of copyrighted books, as well as many older works, would be a significant violation of fair use law.[2] This instructive controversy continued, as Google Print responded by agreeing to provide only short excerpts of copyrighted books online, and to remove books from the Google index, should publishers make such a request.

Although digitization skeptics articulate fears that libraries are likely to become obsolete for most users, who will increasingly conduct all their research while seated at their computers, others argue that libraries are gaining customers from visitors who wish to read hard copies of books encountered online, avail themselves of the potential epiphanies that can be generated by one's physical presence among the stacks, or even use public Internet terminals. Meanwhile, anecdotal evidence and experience suggests that more and more faculty researchers and graduate students complement occasional visits to university and college libraries with an increasing dependence upon online research, a trend to which Google Print is responding. In 1997, a formal plan for incorporating technology into the curriculum existed at only 25 percent of higher education institutions, and only 10 percent of classes used the World Wide Web (Oblinger & Rush, 2000). An emerging strategic and budgetary rule, which appears to be regularly cited by chief information officers, is that an institution should allocate up to 10 percent of its budget to information technology, in order to stay current. However, few universities can report such an expenditure budget.

New production, delivery, and certification organizations have invaded the distribution of higher education courses. The market for distance learning consists mostly of working adults, and was valued at $5 billion in 2004, a 38 percent increase over the preceding year. Universities such as Harvard, Stanford, and Duke currently offer full credit for online courses. More and more faculty members, in disciplinary areas as disparate as the humanities, education, engineering, and the natural sciences, are finding that online course components, if not necessarily complete courses, can enhance student interest and satisfaction with content, as well as faculty ability to engage students in dialogue concerning core concepts, tools, and data. Given the increasingly competitive environment in which institutions find themselves, a key challenge of "sited" education is to make the case for the value of in-person interaction with peers and faculty, and for the socializing and team-development benefits to be gained from having students present themselves at the same time and place repeatedly, for such purposes. Such institutions also need to explain clearly and repeatedly why liberal education provides the core of what it means to be an educated person.

From a university governance perspective, the impact of technology has brought with it a new set of significant challenges for academic decision makers. It raises questions that, for the most part, have no easy answers: Who controls the course content? Who sets the standards for faculty qualifications? How do we accredit these programs? The Council of Regional Accrediting Commissions, which is composed of the six regional accreditation bodies, hired the Western Cooperative for Educational Telecommunication to develop new standards for distance education programs (Carnevale, 2000). The Council, rather than each regional accrediting commission, was charged with this task because distance education programs have potentially unlimited geographical reach. The basic premise of the accreditation guidelines is to use technology to better understand the strengths and weaknesses of individual students, and to focus on student learning. More and more institutions are joining with for-profit companies as well as with other institutions to offer online distance education courses. As with other such strategic alliances or "curricular joint ventures," this can generate significant and continuing conflicts within governance structures on campus, absent the design and implementation of functional business models and work plans by informed and creative campus leaders (Eckel, Affolter-Caine, & Green, 2003).

ECTs have lowered the capital costs of entry into the higher education market through online institutions. Although the initial development costs for multimedia courses can be high—60 percent of the total cost of an online course, over its first five years, is development, rather than delivery related—content can increasingly be sourced externally (Bates, 2000). Where a professor might teach a small class at a direct and indirect cost of some $300.00/hour, online course delivery has a marginal cost of about 3 cents/hour. Even when online tutoring by adjunct faculty is added, the cost is approximately $30.00/hour.

Although instructional technology can minimize capital and operating costs, while maximizing geographical reach, such technology has yet to impel a paradigm shift in teaching, and many faculty members do not incorporate ECTs into their course work. Zemsky and Massy (2004) found that 44 percent of faculty from six institutions, interviewed and observed over a 15-month period, had developed a comprehensive e-learning course; 57 percent required e-mail discussions in their courses; and 91 percent required students to use Web-based materials in class. At the same time, an Eduventures study found that 92 percent of public institutions were now providing distance education courses. One continuing constraint: the lack of a standardized format or software tool for creating online course enhancements.

The governance and funding of higher education have been deeply rooted in the beliefs that college teaching is labor-intensive and best done as a "cottage industry." It is argued that the traditional model of liberal education associated with such an approach fosters both student learning and leadership. In the year 2000, an estimated 40 percent of the Fortune 500 chief executives had graduated from a liberal arts college or received a degree with a major in the liberal arts. As "affinity beings," students enjoy learning among and from other students, in a context of sustained social interaction. Their thoughts and ideas are validated by face-to-face discussion (Durden, 2001). Yet e-learning may not only be a vital tool for the delivery of workplace training and adult continuing education, but also a useful supplement to liberal education. If chat rooms and instant messaging techniques cannot yet mirror small group seminars effectively, instructional technologies continue to evolve. The inherent advantages of traditional liberal arts education remain the values added for 18- to 24-year-old undergraduates in residential environments and the intensive socialization inherent in "learning how to learn," as well as to think critically. Technology is quickly evolving to capture these dimensions. No longer is it akin to reading a book on a screen with its high degree of interactivity and complexity.

E-learning has shifted the cost of education from the delivery side toward the design side, and in turn is changing traditional faculty roles. Educational specialists, who design course structure and focus on the delivery method, rather than the actual content, are becoming more common. Once a course has been designed and delivered to a few students, it can be duplicated in a very cost-effective manner to hundreds, even thousands of other learners, in principle. If the course content belongs to the individual faculty member as his or her intellectual property, a position held by the American Association of University Professors, but the design and delivery belong to the University, who actually owns the "course?" Many universities consider distance courses their property, created by their employees as "work for hire." An industry-wide agreement that the intellectual copyright on course materials is vested in the employing institution, rather than the faculty member, is likely to retard the development of online education, as with restricted accreditation.

A central issue that must be examined by any institution wishing to develop e-learning programs is its intellectual property policy. An effective online distance education policy will establish clear patent, copyright, and software policy statements. This may also involve the use of logo, trademark, or other institutional symbols, such as a campus mascot. Intellectual property rights must establish ownership of the distance education course. What are the institutional and faculty rights and responsibilities after the course is created and offered online? In fact, these issues should be settled well before the course is developed and online.

Most universities will find that distance learning and intellectual property rights cannot be organized into a single statement. For instance, faculty may want to argue that distance education course material should be covered by the university's copyright policy, whereas the financial officer may want to focus on the cost to the institution and argue that such material is covered by the patent policy. Meanwhile, small colleges may not even have such copyright or patent policies in place.

One approach is to offer copyright protection to the creators of a course, while dividing course ownership into content and design. Professors continue to control the actual content. If a faculty member leaves the university, or the course is sold to another institution, the faculty member who generated the content maintains control, receiving royalties and continuing to manage the course's content. This encourages faculty and staff to contribute to online course development. However, the instructional design remains the property of the institution where the course was created. By 2001, such a policy had been adopted by a number of institutions, including the University of Vermont (Carnevale, 2001).

But the underlying dilemma of how best to apportion control and returns from the production and presentation of distance learning courses is by no means fully resolved. Although this ownership policy is faculty-friendly, many questions remain to be answered. Under generally accepted philosophic principles, colleges and universities operate for the common good. Public and private support is based on the perception that colleges and universities deserve financial support because education is beneficial to everyone. If an institution's activities become seen as property that can be sold, has "real" value, and possesses commercial worth, then the public's perception of the university's mission may be compromised (Bérubé, 1996). Stakeholders may question the mission of higher education, and this will inevitably raise questions about the level of support to be provided. However, the business model of online learning, and its implications, may, in time, be countered by open source, freely shared curricula, as exemplified by the Massachusetts Institute of Technology's Open Courseware project.

The U.S. higher education system has accomplished much, not through private gain, not through government regulation, but through governance structures committed to the higher common good, in principle, and usually in practice. Traditionally, student learning and the public interest have been core values within the organizational cultures of every college and university. These objectives have not always been clearly spelled out in mission and vision statements; however, they have usually been at least implicit. By contrast, the pursuit of private institutional and individual gain has become one of the key goals of twenty-first-century higher education.

An underlying premise has been that both the social and private interests served by higher education are important to advance states and the nation. For example, customized research, undertaken by public research universities and subsidized by private businesses, as well as by customized worker training at community colleges and other institutions, helps advance private sector interests. For-profit and revenue-generating ventures have been increasingly spawned from public universities and nonprofit educational institutions. One unintended result may be that the viability and expansion of private alternatives might provide a rationale for diminishing public investment in higher education, as the perceived public good diminishes (Longanecker, 2001). This presents one of the fundamental challenges of university governance in the twenty-first century. E-learning continues to exemplify this challenge.

The private-sector model has often been promoted as appropriate for colleges and universities and as a potential solution to perceived outdated modes of governance. Many board members who come from a corporate background view education as a product and want to govern its "production." From this corporate perspective, higher education is inefficient and cumbersome for employees (faculty) to control product quality and quantity. Indeed, many such board members may have a compulsion to run the college or university as if it were a for-profit corporation. However, faculty and deans generally reject the uncritical application of the corporate model to education. They argue that the academy is not a business where either knowledge or management authority can be centralized, systematized, and easily replicated and produced. Although a place exists for the market in higher education, the market should be kept in its place.

THE IMPACT OF ECTS ON UNIVERSITY AND COLLEGE GOVERNANCE

University governance usually engages the energies and interests of multiple actors, including faculty, administrators, staff, students, trustees, state legislators, departments of education, and accrediting agencies. It is sometimes argued that such extensive involvement tends to generate inertia, which can impede technological change. Yet well-structured institutional governance can encourage information empowerment when a significant degree of decentralized but coordinated decision making is put in place. The distributed client-server model of computing, characterized by individual client units, purchased applications, windowing, and the use of private local area networks or mixed private-public switched networks, is giving way to network-centric computing, changing the dynamics of the types of decisions and involvement required to advance technology change on campus. This new approach requires multisource hardware platforms, software subscriptions rather than purchase, and public switched infrastructure, wired as well as wireless. As generations of computer technology succeed each other with increasing rapidity following these new approaches, the inadequacy of the prototypical twentieth-century structure and process of authoritative university decision making comes into sharper relief.

The implementation of an effective information technology strategy actually implies important adjustments in campus governance, administration, and management. In terms of governance, authoritative or centralized decision-making processes need to be replaced with decision making pushed downward to the lowest competent level, normally the department or program, with clearly specified rewards for teams that achieve defined objectives. Such a strategy requires a relatively flat hierarchy, operational integration, together with the celebration of a culture of achievement and service. Distributed online processing, with common high-speed networking interfaces across college and university campuses, can facilitate this approach (Katz & West, 1992). A "single system image," or natural extension of a given user's native computing environment, free from specific computing and communications protocols, can create the kind of integrated systems architecture that can transform university administration (Gleason, 1991). This would allow administrators using varying kinds of hardware and software to transfer and manipulate files readily, in the course of their daily work, and facilitate authorized access to university databases. However, such changes require the vision, commitment, and encouragement of trustees, presidents, and other senior university leaders. This represents another recurrent aspect of the challenges to governance posed by e-learning, inter alia.

Can college and university governance move toward more effective governance systems, taking the e-learning environment fully into account? Shared governance is not readily associated with entrepreneurship, rapid decision-making, timely market differentiation, and effective distribution channel management, all characteristics of the high-tech marketplace of which higher education is quickly becoming a part. From a university governance perspective, the key questions include resource availability; transparency in resource allocation to ECT; the level of investment in such technologies compared with investment in competing academic priorities, such as financial aid for students and faculty development; the ready "horizontal" as well as "vertical" availability of actionable information; the ability of campus stakeholders to access it; and the extent to which senior administrators, as well as presidents and board members, are willing and able to provide such information, together with requested responses to comments, questions, and concerns, in a timely manner.

A consensual vision as to the potentials of ECT to enhance mission and goal attainment, at the levels of boards of trustees, senior campus executives, administrators, faculty, and other key stakeholders, would be the first step on the way to catalyze action. Such action should ensure that the selected educational and communications technologies add optimal value, rather than introduce new layers of unnecessary operational complexity. A second step would be to review the organization chart and to consider how fewer layers of administration might become practicable, as a result of changing internal communications systems and methods, including the implementation of interactive databases across all major functions. ECTs are extraordinarily transformative tools, to the extent to which their implementation, maintenance, and enhancement are strategically and clearly related to compelling organizational needs.

BEHIND THE E-SCENES AT THE UNIVERSITY OF THE WEST INDIES

The University of the West Indies is one of only two regional universities in the world, in the sense that it serves 15 contributing countries scattered across the Caribbean Sea.[3] In 1983, the University of the West Indies implemented UWIDITE, the UWI Distance Teaching Experiment, with the goal of offering First Year Social Science Certificates in Business, Public Administration, and Education, using an audio teleconferencing system, as part of its Extramural or Continuing Education Program. Students also received supplementary printed materials. In addition, UWI offered outreach and related materials in health, agriculture, and education, while UWIDITE facilitated teleconferenced administrative meetings. The challenges encountered in the course of implementing UWIDITE included faculty training, course design, student motivation, communications equipment quality, hardware and software costs, and effective articulation between distance and classroom education. In 1996, however, following increased emphasis upon the quality of distance education offerings and the development of a strategic plan to make UWI a full dual-mode university, the University decided to rename the program UWIDEC (University of the West Indies Distance Education Center), and the School for Continuing Education was placed under a Director reporting to the Pro Vice-Chancellor for Distance Education and the Non-Campus Countries. Benchmark-related discussions continue as to the operational strategy, funding levels, administrative location, and evaluation of UWIDEC.

Complete degree courses were projected in social science and management, "preliminary sciences" in natural science, together with a Diploma in Education and in Construction Engineering. At that time, there were 25 UWIDEC sites in 14 countries. The intention was to upgrade these sites to allow more efficient two-way communication and to develop a total of 43 such sites, 21 in the "Campus Countries" of Jamaica, Trinidad and Tobago, and Barbados, and 22 in the remaining 12 countries served by UWI, with a total enrollment target of 1,000 FTE. During the 2001–2002 academic year, the University was enrolling 2,200 students and was closing in on its FTE target. By the 2003–2004 academic year, 2,681 students were enrolled in the Distance Education Center, representing 63 percent of all UWI's off-campus students.

The University's 1997–2002 strategic plan also projected the provision of postgraduate degree programs in business administration and the social sciences through UWIDEC, while emphasizing that the academic content of the programs would be under the firm control of the faculties, so that there would be no deviation from the high academic standards viewed as the hallmark of the UWI degree (The University of the West Indies, 1997). It was expected that the cost of delivering distance education courses would be significantly less than the costs of teaching the same courses in the classroom, and that it would eventually be possible to market distance education courses to nonregional institutions.

By 2004, when UWIDEC's primary goals included faculty and student access to a matrix of courses, modules, and learning objects, so as to rapidly construct programs that responded to the changing higher education environment, the most popular certificate and baccalaureate degree programs included agriculture, agribusiness management, economics (level one), education administration, security administration, public administration, management studies, and gender and development studies. During the 2004–2005 academic year, UWIDEC launched an *ACollab Virtual Workspace Project,* driven by open source software, intended to create a shared virtual workspace, so that members of specific communities of practice could share ideas and work collaboratively.

The continuing challenges of effectively using educational and communications technologies at the University of the West Indies include the design and implementation of a comprehensive technology policy, which can facilitate faculty training; the deployment of distance education programs and instructional materials; as well as the management and maintenance of Web delivery systems. It is also necessary to provide for the regular evaluation of existing distance education programs and instructional materials, including research into best practices in distance education.

In addition, a functional interface between the educational technologies represented by the UWI Distance Education Center and the communications technologies represented by the Banner software used for most administrative purposes has yet to be achieved. Cost is a fundamental and continuing concern. For example, faculty and other staff training, as well as equipment maintenance and upgrading, turned out to be so expensive that the envisaged savings from the delivery of distance education courses did not materialize. Furthermore, high-speed Internet connection costs US$400.00 per month in Antigua, Barbados, and Jamaica, compared with approximately US$40.00 in the United States. One result is that regional Internet density remains low, in terms of users per 100 inhabitants, ranging from 5.98 in St. Vincent and the Grenadines to 20 in Jamaica and St. Kitts-Nevis (Escobari, Rabkin, & Rodriguez, 2005). The majority of UWI students do not have access to an Internet-connected computer at home. Other challenges included space and time limitations within UWIDEC for course and tutorial production, as well as student support.

Turning to related regional developments, the Caribbean Knowledge and Learning Network (CKLN) was launched on July 4, 2004, following endorsement by Caribbean Community & Common Market (CARICOM) Heads of Government. It was expected to enhance infrastructure and bandwidth capacity at all 27 UWIDEC Learning Centers. The total estimated cost was $25.6 million, and the potential funding sources identified included the Organization of American States (OAS), Canadian International Development Agency, the European Union, and the Institute for Connectivity in the Americas. A related contract for institutional strengthening was awarded by the OAS through the Association of Caribbean Tertiary Institutions on March 1, 2005.

The goal was to use information and communications technology to strengthen regional tertiary institutions; foster specialization and knowledge sharing; ensure the convergence of fragmented regional and international initiatives to maximize results in the area of tertiary and distance education; and provide a gateway to knowledge resources available elsewhere. The CKLN implementation plan projected the location of an IT Centre of Excellence on the Campus of an existing tertiary education institution, with the objective of building a broad base of highly trained IT professionals in the Caribbean, in partnership with private sector IT companies. However, it has not been possible to interest additional intergovernmental or private sector investors in further implementation of this network, and there is increasing skepticism within the UWI as to when and how it will be possible to move this project forward.

In summation, the continuing challenges of university governance at the UWI with regard to e-learning include its most effective administrative location, the investment of resources that are commensurate with related goals, the engagement of larger numbers of faculty members in training and course development programs, and means of enhancing the quality of its videoconferencing equipment for both management and educational purposes.

CONCLUSION

Educational and communications technologies have transformed the higher education environment. New opportunities to improve university management and governance, as well as research, teaching and learning, have been accompanied by new challenges of data security, cost, intellectual property policy, crisis management, and expectations. Some of these are exemplified by the case of the University of the West Indies, which was summarized in the course of this chapter. Governance structures, shaped and reshaped by technology, in response to its demands, can help to enhance teaching, learning, and research, but the idea of a university is changing to accommodate the potentials of distance and distributed education, the realities of online research, and international as well as interdisciplinary collaboration facilitated by communications technologies. Campus management systems may become more effective, as interactive personnel, payroll, student, financial aid, curricula, and facilities databases are established, but ERP installation costs and time to completion continue to give even some major institutions of higher education pause. ECTs may facilitate horizontal and vertical communication across the campus community, but will not, in themselves, alter the organizational cultures and structures and environmental pressures that have driven many universities and colleges to function more and more like corporations, in terms of leadership recruitment, management style, the roles of faculty and students in nonsymbolic decision making, and the profit imperative.

What will the future hold for higher education? Will enterprise-applications software enhance university management in a cost-effective manner? Will ECTs continue to improve the quality of research, teaching, and learning? Will a new model of shared governance emerge, driven by the increasingly effective use of educational and communications technologies, characterized by flattened hierarchies, and significantly increased operational integration, or will colleges and universities become more like health maintenance organizations, focused upon the provision of standardized services at the lowest possible costs, consistent with targeted profit margins? Will faculty, in a few high-profile cases, become entrepreneurs and superstars, enjoying an international demand for their services, or will most find themselves largely relegated to work similar to that of today's graduate teaching assistants, delivering prepackaged content and grading papers and examinations? These alternatives are not attractive to faculty or senior administrators. Any of these unpleasant futures would fundamentally change the role of faculty in higher education. Questions of academic freedom and quality would be raised, perhaps with serious consequences for public perceptions of higher education. A much more agreeable approach can be found if and when faculty and their institutions shared ownership, and governance, of e-learning programs and courses, much as with patented research, informed by the common understanding that not only the content but the nature of their key governance issues is influenced by changes in technology. What is certain is that ECTs will continue to impact university schedules, processes, and decision arenas in both expected and unexpected ways, and that the quality, cost, and accessibility of related software constitute continuously changing variables as well, affecting the entire educational enterprise, while globally expanding its actual and potential scope.

APPENDIX I: QUESTIONNAIRE—ECTS AND UNIVERSITY GOVERNANCE

1. Are you familiar with the uses of large-scale administrative data base systems such as PeopleSoft, Oracle, Banner and SAP?
2. If so, what do you see as the net advantages of each system, for administrative purposes, such as enrollment, financial and space management?
3. Has one of these systems been installed at your University?
4. If so, how and why was the decision made to select this system?
5. If so, how long was the cost recovery period or how long is it projected to be?
6. What performance measures have you established for this system?[4]
7. How does this system relate to the University's strategic plan?
8. Has this system improved communication between governance participants, including faculty, administrators and staff, across the campus community?

9. Has this system enhanced the quality and speed of management decisions on campus?

10. Does your university make use of educational software such as WebCT, Lotus Notes and Blackboard?

11. If so, how was the decision made to select the software purchased?

12. What performance measures have been established for this software?

13. Is this software helping to enrich the educational experience for traditional as well as non-traditional students?

14. Have you any concluding comments concerning the relationship between educational and communications software and university governance?

NOTES

1. These questionnaires were evenly distributed across the four institutional categories identified.

2. This major project includes libraries at Harvard and Stanford Universities, the University of Michigan at Ann Arbor, the New York Public Library, and the University of Oxford, England.

3. The University of the South Pacific is the other such regional institution.

4. The standard measures include customer satisfaction, organizational and data management flexibility, internal business process improvements, productivity, and cost-effectiveness.

REFERENCES

Bates, A. W. (2000). *Managing technological change*. San Francisco: Jossey-Bass.

Bérubé, M. (1996). Public perceptions of universities and faculty. *Academe, 82*(4), 10–17.

Carnevale, D. (2000, September 21). Accrediting bodies consider new standards for distance-education programs. *The Chronicle of Higher Education*. Retrieved from http://chronicle.com/weekly/v47/i02/02a05801.htm.

Carnevale, D. (2001, May 21). U. of Vermont considers intellectual-property policy said to foster distance education. *The Chronicle of Higher Education*. Retrieved from http://chronicle.com/free/2001/05/2001052401u.htm.

Durden, W. (2001, October 19). Liberal arts for all, not just the rich. *The Chronicle of Higher Education*. Retrieved from http://chronicle.com/weekly/v48/i08/ 08b02001.htm.

Eckel, P., Affolter-Caine, B., & Green, M. (2003). *New times, new strategies: Curricular joint ventures* (The Changing Enterprise Occasional Paper No. 2). Washington, DC: American Council on Education.

Foster, A. (2002, October 15). Louisiana board of regents shuts down four distance learning institutions. *The Chronicle of Higher Education*. Retrieved from http://chronicle.com/weekly/v48/i25/25a03403.htm.

Gleason, B. W. (1991). Open access: A user information system (Professional Paper Series CAUSE6). Boulder, CO: National Center for Higher Education Management Systems.

Escobari, M., Rabkin, D., and Rodriguez, C. (2005, April). Improving competitiveness and increasing economic diversification in the Caribbean: The role of ICT (Information for Development Program Technical Paper Series, Report No. 34306). Retrieved from http://www-wds.worldbank.org/external/default/WDSContent-Server/ IW3P/IB/2005/11/16/000160016_20051116122052/Rendered/PDF/343060LAC0Competitiveness0Growth0ICT.pdf.

Katz, R. N., and West, R. P. (1992). *Sustaining excellence in the 21st century: A vision and strategies for college and university administration* (Professional Paper Series CAUSE8). Boulder, CO: National Center for Higher Education Management Systems.

Kiernan (2005). College spending on technology will decline again this year, a survey suggests. *The Chronicle of Higher Education.* Retrieved September 2, 2005 from http://chronicle.com/prm/daily/2005/02/2005020903n.htm.

Longanecker, D. A. (2001). The public-private balance: Keeping higher education's reason for being in perspective. *American Association for Higher Education (AAHE) Bulletin, 53*(9), 3–4.

Oblinger, D. G., & Rush, S. C. (2000). *The learning revolution: The challenge of information technology in the academy.* Boston: Anker.

United Nations Economic Commission for Latin America and the Caribbean. (2002, April 15). *Globalization and Development* LC/G.2157 (SES.29/3; Table 2.3).Port of Spain, Trinidad: ECLAC.

The University of the West Indies (1997). *Strategic Plan for UWI, 1997–2002.* Kingston, Jamaica: University of the West Indies Press.

Zemsky, R. and Massy, W. (2004). *Thwarted Innovation: What happened to e-learning and why.* A Final Report for The Weatherstation Project of The Learning Alliance at the University of Pennsylvania in cooperation with the Thomson Corporation. Retrieved from: http://www.irhe.upenn.edu/Docs/Jun2004/ThwartedInnovation.pdf.

CHAPTER

Activist Trustees in the University: Reconceptualizing the Public Interest

Michael N. Bastedo
University of Michigan

Inappropriate external influences on a governing board have great potential to skew an institution's priorities and compromise its capacity to serve the public interest. They also may weaken a board's governing integrity by creating imbalances that favor certain interests over others ... the institution is made vulnerable to control by single interests—economic, political, ideological, or professional.
—Association of Governing Boards (AGB, 2001, p. 7)

In most states, the statutory authority for active trusteeship is unmistakable. The passive culture of trusteeship accounts for the fact that many governing boards believe their role is to acquiesce to the wishes of those inside their institutions—without questioning in earnest what is in the best interest of students, taxpayers, or the public at large, and without considering the larger purposes for which their universities exist.
—Phyllis Krutsch, former Regent, University of Wisconsin (1998, p. 24)

Trustee activism has been a hot topic in governance for more than 10 years, and yet it remains a poorly understood phenomenon. Although there has been a great deal of talk in general-interest magazines such as *The Chronicle of Higher Education* and *Trusteeship*, empirical research is only now emerging in the published literature (Bastedo, 2005a). Indeed, the role of external governance is not as well researched as it should be, considering the deep impacts it has on public universities and the changing nature of the social contract between policy makers and higher education (Kezar, 2004; Kezar & Eckel, 2004; Leslie & Novak, 2003; McLendon, 2003a, 2003b). This chapter analyzes the phenomenon of trustee activism, reviews previous discussion of its causes and major interests, and provides a new lens to examine the intentions of the major actors. Later, I will argue that activist trustees see themselves as protectors of a public trust, one that must be reconceptualized in light of what they see as declining academic standards and broad failures of shared governance.

To date, there has been no consistent reasoning on the causes of trustee activism. Chait (1995) and Lazerson (1997) argue compellingly that shareholder activism and the revolution in corporate governance have translated to some extent into the sphere of higher education governance. The agents of this change are the trustees themselves, who in their capacity as CEOs and/or corporate board members in their own right are increasingly comfortable with boards that are constructively critical of the enterprises they oversee. The revolution in corporate governance has also reinforced, in the values and beliefs of trustees, the duties and obligations associated with trusteeship from fiduciary, legal, and public relations perspectives.

James Mingle (1998), the former head of the State Higher Education Executive Officers, argues that the characteristics of board members themselves have changed. "A new breed of board member is being appointed. Board service no longer is a leisure activity for the retired civic or business leader," he says. "Bright, busy, and often ambitious, these new board members want to see some impact from the time and energy they devote to board service." Some argue that these ambitious new board members may be more likely to serve single-interest constituencies or even use these positions as stepping stones for personal political gain (Novak, Leslie, & Hines, 1998).

Public debate, however, has been more clearly focused on the impact of politicized environments, particularly at the state government level. Former Virginia governor James Gilmore recently complained that his attempts to reform Virginia colleges failed because the trustees he appointed "went native" and sided with university administrators (Munro, 2003). Certainly governors and state legislators desire to have increasing influence over the trustees they appoint to state and university governing boards (AGB, 1998). Yet not all agree that policy makers are seeking to create activists in their trustees. "The underlying source is a troubled and self-doubting society that is skeptical and untrusting of *all* of its institutions," argues Richard T. Ingram (1996, p. 53), head of the Association of Governing Boards.

Whatever its source, institutions have emerged to nurture the development of this embryonic movement. In 1995, the National Alumni Forum was co-founded by Lynne Cheney to promote higher academic standards and accountability in higher education through the political mobilization of college and university alumni. Now named the American Council of Trustees and Alumni (ACTA), the group has developed over time as a national voice on governance issues and explicitly seeks to influence the course of higher education through trustee education. In 2003, ACTA opened its Institute for Effective Governance, promising an alternative to the Association of Governing Boards, whom ACTA argues is primarily interested in protecting institutional interests and presidential autonomy. ACTA accepts charitable donations and encourages membership from university governing boards, and offers workshops and other forms of trustee education to its members (ACTA, 2004). Ostensibly bipartisan—ACTA's board includes Senator Joseph I. Lieberman and *New Republic* publisher Martin Peretz—the group has nonetheless been attacked for promoting a right-wing agenda through its attacks on shared governance and calls for established core curricula (Bérubé, 1997; Stimpson, 1998).

POLITICAL CONSERVATISM

Particularly in its early stages, the national press portrayed trustee activism as primarily a political movement designed to promote a right-wing ideology on college campuses. From this perspective, the "Republican Revolution" of 1994, which elected hefty Republican majorities to both houses of Congress, gave new fire to the conservative movement that spilled into higher education governance. "A new group of public-college trustees is moving aggressively to transform the agendas of governing boards and to wipe out what some call 'radical liberalism' on their campuses," said Healy (1996). "What separates these new appointees is their conservative, activist approach to stewardship and policy making. They have much in common with the governors who chose them. Both the governors and the trustees are fiscal and social conservatives, primarily white and male."

Indeed, this perspective can be supported by a number of statements in the conservative press. The editorial page of *The Wall Street Journal*, for example, made this statement in 2001:

> For years now the trustees of many colleges and universities have rolled over as academics and administrators within the institutions they're supposed to govern have run amok. While trustees turned a blind eye, faculty and administrators have politicized and dumbed down the curriculum, instituted draconian speech and sexual-conduct codes that they've enforced with all of the liberalism of the Court of the Star Chamber, and instituted an immoral and often unconstitutional system of admissions apartheid. (WSJ Editorial Board, 2001)

This passage displays both the sparkling language and political conservatism for which *The Wall Street Journal* editorial page is well known. Yet it quickly identifies three of the major criticisms that conservatives have of higher education: declining academic standards, preferential admissions, and "political correctness."

One of the touchstones for activist trustees has been Ward Connerly, the former regent of the University of California and the leader of state movements to eliminate affirmative action. As regent, he persuaded the Board of Regents to pass SP-1, which eliminated the use of race in admissions at the University of California. Connerly subsequently led the battle to pass Proposition 209 in California in 1996 and a decade later is supporting the "Michigan Civil Rights Initiative" with Jennifer Gratz and Barbara Grutter, the litigants in the affirmative action cases against the University of Michigan. Connerly has used his position as a trustee as a platform from which to become a nationally known speaker on issues of race and affirmative action in America. Indeed, he is now the chairman and founder of the American Civil Rights Institute, a not-for-profit organization that exists solely to oppose race and gender preferences.

Recently, there has been sympathy among some in the trustee activism movement for the "Academic Bill of Rights" promoted by conservative columnist David Horowitz. The Academic Bill of Rights would force colleges and universities to ensure that a range of political viewpoints is represented in all campuses and classrooms, through affirmation of the need for "intellectual diversity" in the selection of speakers, classroom topics, and in tenuring junior faculty. Academic Bill of Rights laws are being considered in state legislatures throughout the country. For example, a Florida bill, which passed a committee in its House of Representatives, would establish a student's right to sue professors who do not teach ideas that represent the full range of the political spectrum.

Some in the conservative movement have labeled these demands for intellectual diversity as commensurate with demands for racial, ethnic, and gender diversity. Anne D. Neal, the new head of ACTA, sees this is an opportunity for trustee intervention. "Trustees should direct administrators and faculty to engage in an 'intellectual diversity inventory' to see whether students are exposed to diverse points of view in classroom readings, speakers series, etc., and whether partisan or ideological bias is influencing hiring and retention" (Neal, 2003). Fascinatingly, Neal has specifically employed the same terminology and approach as those who seek to root out other forms of discrimination.

Leftist academics see even more troubling machinations at work, and place trustee activism within a changing national and even global political context. One of the most prominent activist trustees was James F. Carlin, who led the Massachusetts Board of Higher Education from 1995 to 1999 (Bastedo, 2005a; Carlin, 1999). His detractors portray Carlin—a registered Democrat—as an ideological tool of right-wing factions that have assumed power in state legislatures in recent years. "[Carlin] represents the concerted effort on the part of conservative ideologues to dismantle the gains of the welfare state, eliminate public entitlements, and abolish all those public spheres that subordinate civic considerations and noncommercial values to the dictates of an allegedly 'free' market" (Aronowitz & Giroux, 2000, p. 333).

It is not at all clear, however, what forms of political conservatism are in play. "The new paradigm combined business practices and political conservatism," according to Burke (1999, pp. 77–78). "Conservatism contributed distaste for centralized authority, collective planning, and external mandates. In many ways this new decentralization reflects the conservative consensus that has captured Washington and most state capitols." But some elements of decentralization reflecting the actions of activist trustees, such as the use of "carrot and stick" type approaches to policy implementation, may simply be enhancing presidential accountability to statewide governing boards (Bastedo, 2005b). Many observers see trustee activism as primarily a top-down, centralized, and authoritarian approach to governance oversight with political overtones (Lazerson, 1997). Indeed, trustee activists have considerable faith in the ability of government to foment change. It is difficult to find any significant examples of "distaste for centralized authority" in the policy making promoted by these trustees.

Yet there are those on the left who have sympathy for the arguments being made by conservative trustees. "One senses that there are many in and out of academe who might not mind being called activist but who find the language of a James Carlin too crude for their taste. They still perceive deep problems in higher education related to bureaucratic inefficiencies, an unfocused mission, even perhaps a rather unsubstantiated view of academic freedom based on disciplinary integrity," says University of Denver English Professor Eric Gould (2003, pp. 119–120). "One could argue even that if academe were not so good at parodying itself, less swashbuckling techniques from activist trustees might have more bite. But we need to remember that calls for change in higher education are not merely the jeremiads of conservative outsiders."

Many governance experts agree with this assessment. "It would be a mistake to ascribe trustee activism to the Republican landslide of 1994 or to the wishes of any single or small number of conservative state leaders," argues Hines (2000, p. 148). "What is being witnessed now is the confluence of rising public expectations and more conservative attitudes about the institutions of our society in combination with sharpened debate about what higher education should provide to students.... Higher education leaders need to be sensitized to the difference between involvement by politicians as policy leaders and political involvement, which tends to be motivated by political gain."

A key issue is the appointment of new trustees, which many believe has become overly political. From this perspective, public colleges are susceptible to political efforts to change the appointment processes that "favor individuals who may be expected to represent or serve specific views" (AGB, 2001, p. 6). "Such interference often comes from ideological groups that seek not only to influence but also to dictate academic policy by, for example, bypassing governance consultation and collaboration to impose predetermined policies on the institution." These views have been sharply criticized by conservative trustee activists, who see governors and state legislatures as the elected representative of the public interest, and, therefore, appropriately interested in public university governance (ACTA, 2004).

Political interference can create internal board problems as well. Political independence and nonpartisanship are seen by many as the basis by which civil discourse focused on the needs of the institution is built. "If individual trustees become too enmeshed in the political culture of the state while serving on the board, they risk dividing the board along party lines, rendering themselves impotent with members of opposite parties, circumventing the expressed wishes of the whole board, or worst of all, making decisions inimical to the needs of the institution" (Novak, Leslie, & Hines, 1998, p. 29). Thus, from this perspective, overly politicized trustee activism can create long-term problems for the institution, both substantively and politically.

CORPORATE MODELS

Activist trustees have been widely criticized for implementing a number of initiatives that reflect not only political biases but also thrust unduly business-oriented models into university governance. This is not entirely new, of course. In his memoir, Vartan Gregorian describes his encounters with Paul F. Miller, Jr., the new chairman of the University of Pennsylvania board. "We will push hard for evidence of good management on campus," Miller told *The San Francisco Chronicle* in 1979 (Gregorian, 2004, p. 243). "Trustees are the only people in an educational institution that are devoid of self-interest. I firmly believe that management monitoring, as practiced by corporate directors, is perfectly compatible with the educational world." Indeed, Miller may be the first person to be described publicly as an "activist trustee" because of his desire to establish an office on campus.

These kinds of business-oriented approaches are the ones that Chait (1995) and Lazerson (1997) describe following the emergence of shareholder activism and reformation of corporate governance during the 1990s. Chait notes that these changes reflect the realities that corporate directors are increasingly accountable for the outcomes (e.g., profits) produced by business firms. As a result, he sees increasing attention paid to accountability and interest in assessments like graduation exams emerging from this kind of ethos.

Not everyone is sold, however. "Corporate directorship *is* changing, but I would hardly call it a revolution," says Ingram (1996, p. 53). "Most of the major changes in corporate directorship are far from being relevant to academic boards, and the foment in some corporate boardrooms is neither the source nor the cause of academic trustee restlessness." One recent change that has made a great impression on trustees, however, is the Sarbanes-Oxley legislation that emerged following the collapse of Enron and the scandals at Tyco and Worldcom. Sarbanes-Oxley requires corporations to enact a set of financial accountability and governance mechanisms to prevent the kinds of mismanagement that led to those famous debacles. Increasingly, trustees see adherence to the principles of trustee independence and legal liability applying to higher education boards as well (Dreier, 2005).

Somewhat counterintuitively, Chait (1995) also sees the revolution in corporate governance leading to increasing influence for external constituencies:

> Acclimated to the reality that the corporate board can no longer defensibly deny a request to meet with institutional investors on the ground that such sessions erode the lines of authority, trustees will be far more disposed to meet with student and faculty leaders. In today's climate, would trustees dare decline a request, submitted by a coalition of parents concerned about tuition increases, to meet with the finance committee of the board? ... As with corporate boards, the niceties of conventional protocols are likely to yield to the new realities of governance and the redistribution of power. (pp. 15–16)

As a result, Chait argues, there will be a mechanism by which boards of trustees—and, therefore, colleges and universities more broadly—become increasingly sensitive to their environment and to various constituencies. Yet over the past 10 years, one searches to find examples where campus constituent groups have organized themselves as effectively as shareholder or institutional investor activists in business firms.

For many left-leaning faculty, the influence of corporate models has been one of the most negative impacts of trustee activism, and James F. Carlin, the former Massachusetts board chairman, was once again the focus of criticism. "Carlin believes that higher education, like the corporations, should be subject to reorganization and accountability schemes, a strategy that quickly translates into a series of flawed policies designed to cripple the intellectual and economic freedom of faculty" (Giroux, 2000, p. 51). These criticisms delineate sharp and highly simplistic dichotomies that make firms the locus of "reorganization and accountability schemes" and universities the only place for "intellectual and economic freedom." Both conceptualizations need more refined consideration.

This perspective also routinely fails to distinguish between the *rhetoric* of activist trustees and the *policies* that are actually developed and implemented. The rhetoric of trustees such as Carlin, Ward Connerly, and SUNY's Candace de Russy can be as harsh as *The Wall Street Journal* editorial page and just as loud. These trustees are deeply frustrated with issues surrounding such hot-button topics as tenure, political correctness, and affirmative action, and this leads to equally passionate responses, particularly regarding the quality and necessity of faculty research programs (Carlin, 1999). "Carlin's anti-intellectualism and animosity toward educators and students alike is simply a more extreme example of the forces at work in the corporate world that would like to take advantage of the profits to be made in higher education, while simultaneously refashioning colleges and universities in the image of the new multi-national conglomerate landscape" (Giroux, 2003, pp. 175–176).

But we need to distinguish—as Carlin always told his associates—between efforts and results. Carlin's effort to dismantle faculty tenure failed, and he was deeply disappointed by the "toothless" post-tenure review processes that were implemented as a compromise (Carlin, 1999). Candace de Russy made a great deal of hay out of the women and sexuality conference at SUNY–New Paltz in 1999, but no faculty or administrators were let go or even admonished. And although Connerly was successful in passing SP-1, ultimately, the decisions in the Michigan cases support the continued use of racial and ethnic preferences in college admissions.

FACULTY CONTROL

For many activist trustees, one of the primary problems facing higher education is faculty control over work environments, employment conditions, and performance measurement. Trustee activism on these issues is seen by many as arising from corporate conceptions of the appropriate role of workers or employees, ignorance about the faculty role, and a lack of respect for the nature of professional work.

> If many trustee appointments become politicized and boards get very aggres-
> sive in their demands for "more efficient" academic management, we could
> see great pressure not only on administrative functions but also on traditional
> forms of academic organization, personnel and curricular decision making, and
> resource allocation, with the faculty's role substantially circumscribed. Direct
> threats to academic freedom are also possible. (Zumeta, 2001, p. 163)

These concerns question not only the efficiency demands of activist trustees, but also get at the heart of the teaching and learning enterprise. This is particularly true regarding the use of performance measurement to assess student learning outcomes and faculty productivity.

> This is reminiscent of the directive that is coming down from the Massachusetts
> Board of Higher Education that community college faculty produce a list of
> student proficiencies that must be attained by the time of graduation. How far
> away are we from a mandate that these proficiencies, *that faculty, themselves,*
> *have designed,* be made measurable by standardized tests? Then, how far away
> are we from looking back to see that we have been duped into participating
> in our own and our students' defeat, as faculty performance is evaluated by our
> students' achievement or lack of achievement? (Kiefson, 2004, p. 148)

For most people—members of the public included—the idea that faculty should be insulated from evaluation of their students' "achievement or lack of achievement" is patently ridiculous. But one of the most fascinating outcomes of reviewing faculty commentary on trustee activism is how it is primarily focused on parochial concerns about faculty job security and employment conditions. Student impact may be considered, but largely as background to an overall story of faculty victimization. It is not hard to see how activist trustees see faculty as largely out for themselves. "Trustees and administrators must provide bold, innovative solutions—in spite of faculty members' objections, and even if, in the short term, those changes run contrary to the faculty's economic interests" (Carlin, 1999). Faculty lose a great deal of legitimacy by ceding the high ground of public interest to narrow self-interest.

STANDARDS

Any discussion of academic standards or program productivity by trustees is often construed as undue influence into faculty purview of the curriculum (Stimpson, 1998). For activist trustees, however, academic policy is one of the primary responsibilities of conscientious trusteeship, both morally and in their role as institutional fiduciaries.

> Great public costs—fiscal, academic, and goodwill—have been incurred when
> quiescent governing boards have deferred to those who shortened academic
> calendars, reduced teaching loads and general education requirements, paid
> insufficient attention to increases in time and credits to degree, and allowed
> mission creep. Further costs were meted out by those who presided over the
> proliferation of a curricular and organizational structure that wrongly favored

the interests of those who teach instead of favoring what students should know and be able to do when they graduate. (Krutsch, 1998, p. 25)

This has been the major issue pursued by Candace de Russy during her time as a trustee at SUNY. "Trustees need not apologize for seeking to encourage high academic standards and for more closely monitoring academic performance," she writes (de Russy, 1996, p. 10). "Academic freedom does not preclude broad, constructive academic oversight by trustees."

SHARED GOVERNANCE

For Marvin Lazerson (1997), the key to providing a constructive solution to the problem of activist trusteeship lies in resuscitating shared governance. He offers a set of practical options for campus presidents who are facing problems of trustee independence:

> A resuscitated shared governance would give presidents greater protection from the most extreme demands of marauding trustees. Some presidents have begun to recognize this. Taking a page out of the trustee's play book, they are giving to faculty the same hard data they now provide trustees, engaging faculty in their presidential cabinets, coaching faculty on how to talk with trustees, and bringing trustees and faculty together in more honest ways than before, when faculty "show and tell" was the order of the day. (p. 15)

He notes, however, that "faculty have difficulty defining and working toward common goals. One businessman I know who served on an otherwise all-faculty strategic planning committee was shocked at the individualistic nature of the conversations. It was, he said, as if the primary purpose of the institution was to serve each individual faculty member."

As a result, it often falls to presidents and senior administrators to argue that there is often a confluence between what is perceived as faculty self-interest and the appropriate needs of an effective university. Faculty demands for additional resources, for example, may lead to further research that stimulates knowledge and economic development. Faculty whose lives are embedded in disciplines and academic programs are often better suited to make decisions about the future of the curriculum, which shapes the knowledge that will be imparted to society. Yet these concerns can be seen as faculty simply defending their turf or protecting their privileges. Reframing these issues from faculty self-interest to public interest produces a more even playing field—at the level of ideas and politics—and enhances the legitimacy of faculty concerns with activist trustees and other policy makers.

COMPETING CONCEPTIONS OF THE PUBLIC INTEREST

The kinds of interactions between trustees and faculty described by Lazerson lead activist trustees to see themselves as the primary defenders of the public interest within the university. "Trustees who act vigorously to safeguard the public interest—*activist* trustees—will be the most credible and effective advocates and protectors of their institutions in the years ahead" (de Russy, 1996, p. 10). This view is supported by ACTA. "The American Council of Trustees and Alumni believes that it is the obligation of governors to appoint trustees who will represent the public interest, not just advocate for their institutions. This is a trend not to be denounced, but to be honored" (Martin, 2003).

According to a national survey of state policy makers in both governor's offices and legislatures, this conceptualization of trusteeship may have a great deal of political support.

> Virtually every political leader we interviewed agrees that governing boards must balance their roles as advocates for the institution and as guardians of the public trust. Most do not think the public university boards are achieving an appropriate balance. They say boards are favoring the role of "institutional advocate" in favor of "guardian of the public trust." (Ruppert, 1998, p. 75)

If policy makers see faculty and administrators abdicating these roles, they are likely to support trustees who decide to step into the vacuum, particularly on issues that have a great deal of public support. At the same time, legislators remain conflicted about the appropriate role of trustees as a "change agent"—those in more politicized contexts see trustees as overly intrusive, while those from less politicized contexts would like trustees to have a firmer hand. What policy makers want from governance is an appropriate *balance* between institutional and public interests.

This is supported by reports sponsored by the Association of Governing Boards, but there is no consistent message about which interest should take priority. In *Pursuing the Public's Agenda*, for example, MacTaggart and Mingle (2002, p. 12) say that effective governance structures "foster close ties between a governor's office and a state or system board, but ensure enough distance so that the university or system does not become a state agency." How that distance should be defined is not clear. "To deliver for the people of their states, trustees must believe that a public agenda, however defined, is more important than academic self-interest," MacTaggart and Mingle argue. This would lead you to believe that public college trustees are primarily responsible to the public interest rather than to institutional interest. Most AGB documents, however, make it clear that institutional interests must and should come first. "The ultimate responsibility for the institution rests in its governing board. Boards cannot delegate their fiduciary responsibility for the academic integrity and financial health of the institution" (AGB, 1998, p. 3). It would be understandable if trustees leave conversations like this confused about the appropriate balance of priorities.

Activist trustees have no such confusion. They see themselves primarily working for students, taxpayers, and the public interest. Carlin said publicly that he never went to sleep without thinking about how he could reduce the cost of college to students (Bastedo, 2005a). For de Russy, the public interest lies primarily in the establishment of academic standards and the elimination of extravagance or waste. That, in turn, meant that she did not see her role as helping to provide additional resources for the institution to expand or grow.

> In fulfilling those fiduciary responsibilities, it is not necessarily in the interest of the public or the institution for trustees reflexively to press for ever-higher government subsidies for the colleges and universities they oversee, even though some administrators and faculty members see that as the trustees' primary responsibility. (de Russy, 1996, p. 7)

If this type of thinking became common among trustees, it would be truly revolutionary—and potentially highly damaging to the fiduciary health of public institutions. It seems important to consider, however, how inconsistent such an approach is with the corporate models discussed earlier. This is notable for many reasons. First, we need to consider that many of these logics about standards, the public interest, and faculty roles can work in concert or in competition. Simply labeling an idea or approach "activist" does not mean it will be widely accepted. Second, there is not necessarily a consistency in ideas among activist trustees. Carlin, for example, happily oversaw substantial increases in appropriations for Massachusetts colleges during his tenure as board chairman—his primary concern was lowering the cost of education to *students*, not the state (Carlin, 1997a, 1997b). Connerly, for his part, has not shown substantial leadership on any of these issues, while Carlin declares himself a "mild supporter" of affirmative action. How these trustees define the public interest remains as contested as it is for those who reside within higher education.

IMPLICATIONS

If the concept of the public interest remains contested, the real issue of activist trusteeship is not academic standards or tenure or any other specific policy problem. The issue is *how* these preferences are expressed by activist trustees and what these preferences mean for the power dynamic among faculty, administrators, and trustees. It is no coincidence that each side routinely accuses each of the others of arrogance and indifference to the real problems facing the university.

For various historical and organizational reasons, faculty and campus presidents have largely abdicated any role they have played in debates over the public's interest in higher education. (My own university is a notable exception in debates over affirmative action.) The story is familiar: The demands upon campus presidents to continually seek new sources of revenue and to remain sensitive to touchy political environments make engaging the public interest a reluctantly low priority. Prestige-seeking faculty at elite universities are increasingly specialized and research-driven; faculty at lower-ranked universities are increasingly underpaid and overworked, leading to unionization, the increased used of adjuncts as contingent labor, and other forms of deprofessionalization (Rhoades, 1998). One of the few constituencies that may have the time in the university to engage in public interest debates are the trustees, who are often retired, independently wealthy, or both.

Critiques of trustee activism have tended to focus on the implications of trustees' *rhetoric* on faculty employment conditions and job security, overlooking real changes in *policy* that will have far more long-term impacts on the university and society. In particular, if one looks at policies that are actually passed and implemented by boards dominated by activist interests, there is a distinct pattern: the policies tend to increase the inequality of students and institutions in the public higher education system (Bastedo, 2003, 2005b; Bastedo & Gumport, 2003; Gumport & Bastedo, 2001). Policies to increase admissions standards and reduce remedial education at four-year colleges serve to increase the legitimacy of the system with policy makers, but also to concentrate students in the community college system. This "cascading" effect will ultimately reduce baccalaureate attainment in society because of the lower probability of graduating after attending a community college (Dougherty, 1994); and it will be no surprise that the students who are cascaded down the higher education system are disproportionately minority and low-income (Bastedo, 2003; Perna, et al., 2005). In Massachusetts, more than three-quarters of the Latino students in the public higher education system attend community colleges (Bastedo, 2003).

Focusing attention on the rhetoric of activist trustees about tenure, accountability, speech codes, faculty productivity, and gender studies is ultimately a distraction unless this rhetoric is translated into actual policy. These more extreme changes in the higher education system—ones that would require real intrusion into the domains of faculty and presidents—are heavily mitigated by the political environment, the realities of university complexity, and the role of staff in policy development (Bastedo, 2005a). Tenure is a good example; widely unpopular among the public at large, tenure would seem to be easy pickings for an activist trustee seeking to control the faculty, reduce costs, and increase managerial flexibility. But reality quickly intrudes—any university that eliminates tenure will be at an immediate competitive disadvantage, and the cost of "buying out" the tenure of thousands of faculty is clearly prohibitive. Faculty unionization is an extremely powerful barrier to change. Although faculty may feel less powerful and respected than in prior years, they are far more influential than students who, to date, lack the political connections and resources to wield real power.

Pushing back against the trend to make trustees more politicized is nonetheless an important step toward balanced and effective governance. To make trustee appointments less ideological, the Association of Governing Boards is promoting the idea of bipartisan, merit selection of trustees (AGB, 2003). A pilot project in collaboration with Virginia's Governor Mark Warner has been a well-publicized success, and he has made it a priority to institutionalize the process through statute prior to the end of his term. The goal of AGB's initiative is to encourage a thoughtful appointment process that results in the selection of "seasoned partners well qualified to serve the public trust" (Johnson & Clark, 2003). But those in favor of activist trusteeship remain skeptical of these proposals. "If this had been written about a Fortune 500 company, it would sound a lot like code for someone who's not going to ask uncomfortable questions about the corporate jet" (WSJ Editorial Board, 2003).

The definition of merit for trustee appointments will, of course, be politically constructed and evolve over time. The problem is that the proper role of trustees—the appropriate balance between public and institutional interests—has yet to be resolved. Considering the wide range of actors and interests in governance, a complete consensus hardly seems possible. We might also consider whether the trustees that faculty and administrators find the most distasteful would or would not survive a state-level "merit selection" process. Merit selection of trustees may do many things—increase legitimacy and credibility, make it clear to governors that the appointment of trustees is a special and important process—but it seems unlikely to screen out those who may become activists.

CONCLUSION

Given the contested nature of the public interest, trends in corporate governance, the importance and impact of the higher education credential, and the increasingly politicized environment for higher education, there is no reason to believe that trustee activism will depart anytime soon. This will be particularly true for those institutions—flagship public institutions, especially—where flashpoint issues of social, moral, and political importance are likely to be in play. It will be the job of campus presidents and senior administrators to try and mitigate the most negative institutional effects of this behavior, but also to give serious and thoughtful consideration to the concerns being raised. But it will be the job of all of us in higher education—researchers, faculty, students, and administrators alike—to closely monitor the policy responses to trustee activism and measure the impact they have on universities and society.

REFERENCES

American Council of Trustees and Alumni. (2004). *The basics of responsible trusteeship* [Pamphlet]. Washington, DC: Author.

Aronowitz, S., & Giroux, H. A. (2000). The corporate university and the politics of education. *Educational Forum, 64*, 332–339.

Association of Community College Trusteeship. (2001). *The political nature of community college trusteeship*. Washington, DC: Author.

Association of Governing Boards. (1998). *AGB statement on institutional governance*. Washington, DC: Author.

Association of Governing Boards. (2001). *Governing in the public interest: External influences on colleges and universities*. Washington, DC: Author.

Association of Governing Boards. (2003). Merit screening of citizens for gubernatorial appointment to public college and university trusteeship. AGB State Policy Brief No. 1. Washington, DC: AGB.

Bastedo, M. N. (2003, November 12–13). *Cascading minority students in higher education: Assessing the impact of statewide admissions standards*. Paper presented at the ASHE Forum on Public Policy in Higher Education, Association for the Study of Higher Education, Portland, OR.

Bastedo, M. N. (2005a). The making of an activist governing board. *Review of Higher Education, 28*, 551–570.

Bastedo, M. N. (2005b, April 11–15). *Metapolicy: Institutional change and the rationalization of public higher education.* Paper presented at the Annual Meeting of the American Educational Research Association, Montreal, Canada.

Bastedo, M. N., & Gumport, P. J. (2003). Access to what? Mission differentiation and academic stratification in U.S. public higher education. *Higher Education, 46*, 341–359.

Bérubé, M. (1997, February 27). *Faculty psychology for the 21st century.* Invited address to the University Faculty Senate, City University of New York.

Burke, J. J. (1999). Multicampus systems: The challenge of the nineties. In G. H. Gaither (Ed.), *The multicampus system: Perspectives on practice and prospects* (pp. 40–81). Sterling, VA: Stylus.

Carlin, J. F. (1997a, August 10). Why community colleges should be free. *The Boston Globe*, p. B1.

Carlin, J. F. (1997b, November 4). *I know my campus is broken, but if I try to fix it, I'll lose my job.* Address to the Greater Boston Chamber of Commerce.

Carlin, J. F. (1999, November 5). Restoring sanity to an academic world gone mad. *The Chronicle of Higher Education*, p. A76.

Chait, R. P. (1995). *The new activism of corporate boards and the implications for campus governance* (AGB Occasional Paper No. 26). Washington, DC: Association of Governing Boards.

de Russy, C. (1996, November/December). In defense of activist trusteeship. *Trusteeship, 4*(6), 6–10.

Dougherty, K. (1994). *The contradictory college.* Albany: SUNY Press.

Dreier, A. E. (2005, July 8). Sarbanes-Oxley and college accountability. *The Chronicle of Higher Education*, p. B10.

Giroux, H. A. (2000). *Impure acts: The practical politics of cultural studies.* New York: Routledge.

Giroux, H. A. (2002). Neoliberalism, corporate culture, and the promise of higher education: The university as a democratic public sphere. *Harvard Educational Review, 72*, 425–463.

Giroux, H. A. (2003). *The abandoned generation: Democracy beyond the culture of fear.* New York: Palgrave Macmillan.

Gould, E. (2003). *The university in a corporate culture.* New Haven, CT: Yale University Press.

Gregorian, V. (2004). *The road to home: My life and times.* New York: Simon & Schuster.

Gumport, P. J., & Bastedo, M. N. (2001). Academic stratification and endemic conflict: Remedial education policy at the City University of New York. *Review of Higher Education, 24*, 333–349.

Healy, P. (1996, January 26). Newly appointed trustees stir up public colleges. *The Chronicle of Higher Education*, p. A26.

Hines, E. R. (2000). The governance of higher education. *Higher Education: Handbook of Theory and Research, 15*, 105–155.

Ingram, R. T. (1996). New tensions in the academic boardroom. *Educational Record, 77*(2/3), 49–55.

Johnson, N. C., & Clark, C. S. (2003, June 6). Taking the gamesmanship out of appointments to public colleges' governing boards. *The Chronicle of Higher Education*, p. B20.

Kezar, A. (2004). Obtaining integrity? Reviewing and examining the charter between higher education and society. *Review of Higher Education, 27*, 429–459.

Kezar, A., & Eckel, P. D. (2004, July/August). Meeting today's governance challenges: A synthesis of the literature and examination of a future agenda for scholarship. *Journal of Higher Education, 75*, 371–399.

Kiefson, R. (2004). The politics and economics of the super-exploitation of adjuncts. In M. Bousquet, T. Scott, & L. Parascondola (Eds.), *Tenured bosses and disposable teachers: Writing instruction in the managed university* (pp. 143–152). Carbondale: Southern Illinois University.

Krutsch, P. M. (1998, March/April). The passive culture of public boards. *Trusteeship 6(2)*, 22–25.

Lazerson, M. (1997, March/April). Who owns higher education? The changing face of governance. *Change*, 10–15.

Leslie, D. W., & Novak, R. (2003). Substance versus politics: Through the dark mirror of governance reform. *Educational Policy, 17*, 98–129.

MacTaggart, T. J., & Mingle, J. R. (2002). *Pursuing the public's agenda: Trustees in partnership with state leaders*. Washington, DC: Association of Governing Boards.

Martin, J. L. (2003, July 25). Governors who act in the public interest [Letter to the editor]. *The Chronicle of Higher Education*, p. B14.

McLendon, M. K. (2003a). Setting the governmental agenda for the state decentralization of higher education. *Journal of Higher Education, 74*, 479–515.

McLendon, M. K. (2003b). State governance reform of higher education: Patterns, trends, and theories of the public policy process. *Higher Education: Handbook of Theory and Research, 18*, 57–144.

Mingle, J. R. (1998). The new activism of state and system boards. *Trusteeship, 6(2)*, 34.

Munro, N. (2003, October 11). Keeping college trustees on course. *National Journal*, p. 3132.

Neal, A. (2003, October). *Intellectual diversity endangered*. Testimony before the U.S. Senate Committee on Health, Education, Labor, and Pensions, Washington, DC.

Novak, R., Leslie, D., & Hines, E. (Eds.). (1998). *Bridging the gap between state government and public higher education*. Washington, DC: Association of Governing Boards.

Perna, L. W., et al. (2005). State public policies and the racial/ethnic stratification of college access and choice in the state of Maryland. *Review of Higher Education, 28*, 245–272.

Rhoades, G. (1998). *Managed professionals: Unionized faculty and restructuring academic labor*. Albany: State University of New York Press.

Ruppert, S. S. (1998). The views of state political leaders on strengthening public university governance and trusteeship. In R. Novak, D. Leslie, & E. Hines (Eds.), *Bridging the gap between state government and public higher education* (pp. 72–90). Washington, DC: Association of Governing Boards.

Stimpson, C. R. (1998, January 16). Activist trustees wield power gone awry. *The Chronicle of Higher Education*, p. B4.

WSJ Editorial Board. (2001, February 26). Trust the trustees. *The Wall Street Journal*, p. A22.

WSJ Editorial Board. (2003, August 1). In trustees we trust. *The Wall Street Journal*, p. W15.

Zumeta, W. (2001). Public policy and accountability in higher education: Lessons from the past and present for the new millennium. In D. Heller (Ed.), *The states and public higher education policy: Affordability, access, and accountability* (pp. 155–197). Baltimore: Johns Hopkins University Press.

INDEX

ABOUT THE EDITOR AND CONTRIBUTORS

Michael N. Bastedo is Assistant Professor in the Center for the Study of Higher and Postsecondary Education at the University of Michigan. In 2005–2006, he studied European Union policy as a Fulbright Scholar in the Netherlands, and served as an Associate at the National Center for Public Policy and Higher Education. He is Research Director of the Institutes on Public University Governance, supported by the Mellon Foundation and the Carnegie Corporation of New York. His scholarly interests are in public policy, governance, and organization of public higher education. His work has been published in *Review of Higher Education*, *Higher Education*, and *American Higher Education in the 21st Century* (2nd ed.), and is forthcoming in *The New England Journal of Public Policy* and *The Sociology of Higher Education*. Prior to entering the academic profession, Dr. Bastedo held policy positions with the Massachusetts Board of Higher Education, and research positions in the National Center for Postsecondary Improvement and the Stanford Institute for Higher Education Research. He holds the AB with honors from Oberlin College, an MA with distinction from Boston College, and the AM in Sociology and PhD in Administration and Policy Analysis from Stanford University.

Jared Bleak is Managing Director at Duke Corporate Education, a subsidiary of Duke University. In this role, he designs and delivers educational programs for corporate executives and teaches on leadership and governance issues. His research centers on organizational culture and the intersection of education and business. Bleak is the author of *When For-Profit Meets Nonprofit: Educating through the Market*, published by Routledge Falmer. He holds a doctorate from Harvard University.

Peter D. Eckel is Director, Programs and Initiatives, in the American Council on Education's Center for Effective Leadership. He directs a new leadership agenda, focusing on chief academic officers, including the yearlong Institute for New Chief Academic Officers. He additionally oversees a set of projects that explores the leadership challenges of the strategies colleges and universities are pursuing to respond to increased competition and changing fiscal realities. His scholarship addresses questions of policy and practice that hinder and facilitate the effectiveness of colleges and universities, with an emphasis on governance, administration, organization, and the external environment. His research appears in many of the leading peer-reviewed higher education journals, and he is the lead author of three ACE Occasional Paper series: *On Change, The Changing Enterprise,* and *The Changing Relationships between States and Institutions.* He is also series editor of the ACE paper series, *The Unfinished Agenda: Ensuring Success for Students of Color.* His books include *Taking the Reins: Transformation in Higher Education* (with Adrianna Kezar); *Changing Course: Eliminating Academic Programs;* and *Bridging the Gap between Research and Practice in Higher Education* (with Adrianna Kezar). He received his PhD in Education Policy, Planning, and Administration from the University of Maryland, College Park.

Dennis J. Gayle is Senior Advisor to the Chancellor, as well as Vice Chancellor, of the University of the West Indies; Executive Director of the UWI Graduate Institute of International Relations; Professor of Strategic International Business; and Chair, Board of Governors, the University College of the Caribbean. He was educated at the University of the West Indies' Mona Campus, Oxford University, the London School of Economics and Political Science, and the University of California at Los Angeles. Ambassador Gayle served in several capitals, during the 1970s, as a senior diplomatic officer, and participated in a range of major international economic conferences. He was a 1997–1998 Fellow of the American Council on Education, and a 2001 Graduate of Harvard University's Institute of Educational Management. He has also served as Associate Vice President for Academic Affairs at the University of North Florida, and International Center University Director at Florida International University. He has published six books, including *Governance in the Twenty-First-Century University: Approaches to Effective Leadership and Strategic Management* (2003), as well as contributed many book chapters and journal articles.

Matthew Hartley teaches in the higher education management program at the University of Pennsylvania. His research and writing focus on academic governance and organizational change at colleges and universities. He is especially interested in the role that mission plays in shaping new programs and policies. His current research examines how colleges and universities have attempted to advance a particular academic purpose—civic engagement. Dr. Hartley's recent publications include "The Elusive Ideal: Civic Learning and Higher Education" in S. Fuhrman and M. Lazerson (Eds.), *The Public Schools: The Institutions of*

American Democracy Series, 2005 (with Elizabeth Hollander); "Putting Down Roots in the Groves of Academe: The Challenges of Institutionalizing Service-Learning" in D. Butin (Ed.), *Service-Learning in Higher Education: Critical Issues and Directions* (with Ira Harkavy and Lee Benson); "An Endless Good Argument: An Analysis of the Adaptation of Institutional Mission at Two Liberal Arts Colleges and Implications for Decision Making" in *Planning in Higher Education*, 2005 (with Lawrence Schall). He earned an EdM and EdD from Harvard University's Graduate School of Education. His dissertation examined how three liberal arts colleges redefined and implemented new educational missions. Prior to his work at the University of Pennsylvania, he was an instructor for Hobart and William Smith Colleges as well as a teaching fellow and research assistant at Harvard University. He also served as co-chair of the editorial board for *Harvard Educational Review*.

Adrianna Kezar is Associate Professor for Higher Education and Associate Director for the Center for Higher Education Policy Analysis at the University of Southern California. She holds a PhD and MA in higher education administration from the University of Michigan and a BA from the University of California, Los Angeles. She was formerly Assistant Professor at the University of Maryland and George Washington University. Her research focuses on governance, change, leadership, organizational theory, and diversity issues in higher education. Kezar was editor of the *ASHE-ERIC Higher Education Report Series*. She has published more than 75 articles and books and is featured in the major journals for higher education, including *Review of Higher Education*, *Journal of Higher Education*, *Research in Higher Education*, and *Journal of College Student Development*. Her most recent books are *Higher Education for the Public Good* and *Creating Organizational Learning in Higher Education*. Kezar serves as a board member for Project Kaleidoscope and the Association of American Colleges and Universities' *Peer Review*, and has served as a board member for the American Association for Higher Education, Knowledge Network; National TRIO Clearinghouse; and the American Council on Education's CIRP Research Cooperative.

William T. Mallon is Assistant Vice President and Director of Organization and Management Studies at the Association of American Medical Colleges (AAMC), where he conducts research on faculty work life, organizational studies, and leadership in academic medicine and higher education. A recipient of the Dissertation of the Year Citation of Excellence from the Association for the Study of Higher Education (ASHE), Mallon received his doctorate in higher education policy from Harvard University. Prior to joining the AAMC, he was a researcher at the Harvard Project on Faculty Appointments. His most recent publications focus on management, organization, and leadership of academic medical centers. He has published in journals such as *Science*, *Academic Medicine*, and *New Directions in Higher Education*. He is author of *The Handbook of Academic Medicine: How Medical Schools and Teaching Hospi-*

tals Work; Tenure on Trial: Case Studies of Change in Faculty Employment Policies; and "Why Is Tenure One College's Problem and Another's Solution?" in *The Questions of Tenure.* He currently is the principal investigator of a study examining the growth and management of interdisciplinary research centers and institutes, funded by the Burroughs Wellcome Fund. Mallon is a frequent speaker to academic medicine and higher education organizations.

Simi R. Wilhelm Shah is completing a PhD in Higher Education Management at the University of Pennsylvania. Her dissertation research explores the negotiation of the relationships between corporate entities and universities and the influence of such relationships on academic values and governance.